A Taste of Wintergreen

A Taste of Wintergreen

by Lindy Mechefske

WINTERGREEN STUDIOS PRESS
Township of South Frontenac
Ontario, Canada

Wintergreen Studios Press
P.O. Box 75, Yarker, ON, Canada K0K 3N0

Canadian Cataloguing in Publication Data
A Taste of Wintergreen

ISBN: 978 0-9865473-2-4
Mechefske, Lindy, 1961–

I.   Title.

Legal Deposit – Library and Archives Canada 2011

Book design by R. Upitis
Cover photo of garlic scapes by L. Mechefske
Photos by L. Mechefske unless otherwise noted

This book is dedicated to my family: Chris, Laura, and Elysia.
And to Rena Upitis, who had the vision for Wintergreen in the first place,
and who inspired me to take flight in so many ways.

Contents

A Note About Standardized Ingredients and Measurements

Beans

As both a time- and energy-saving measure, we often use canned beans. We try to use BPA-free tins wherever available. Check your local health food store, or the organic section of most major supermarkets. With the exception of baked beans, we always rinse canned beans several times. If you prefer to use dried beans, here is the standard procedure for replicating the contents of one 19 oz (540 ml) can of beans. Soak one cup of beans for 5 hours or overnight. Soaking the beans helps to break down the starches that cause gas and indigestion. Rinse well. Cover with fresh cold water, bring to boil, reduce heat to simmer and skim off impurities. Cook until tender, approximately 45 minutes to 1 hour. Strain and allow the beans to cool before using.

Cilantro and Coriander

Fresh coriander and fresh cilantro are the same thing. In Canada, the fresh herb is typically labeled as cilantro. Depending on where the recipe originates, you will notice it might be called one or the other.

Eggs

We use free-range farm eggs supplied by local farmers. The eggs vary in size but we compensate for extra-small eggs by using more. It would be a safe bet to assume that large or extra-large eggs would suffice wherever eggs are called for.

Flour

Unless otherwise specified, we use unbleached, organic, all-purpose flour.

Yoghurt

Unless otherwise specified, we use full-fat Greek-style yoghurt.

Measurement Units

Please note that we have used the curious mixture of Metric and Imperial measurements, as is commonly the case in Canada. The Canadian norm is to use teaspoons, cups, and Fahrenheit oven temperatures, along with baking pans listed with Imperial measurements. On the other hand, many consumables are sold by both Metric and Imperial measures, so where possible, we have included both sets of measurements. For some items (e.g., anchovies) only Metric measurements are given because they are only sold in Canada with Metric measurements listed.

Preface

The art of dining well is no slight art, the pleasure not a slight pleasure.

~ Michel de Montaigne (1533–1592)
French writer and father of Modern Skepticism

Wintergreen Studios, an environmental and arts education eco-retreat centre, sits on a couple of hundred pristine acres on the Canadian Shield, land that forms part of the UNESCO world heritage site known as the Frontenac Arch Biosphere Reserve. An hour north of Kingston, Ontario, *The New York Times* once nominated the area as one of the ten best places in North America to buy land.

"Rugged, complicated land," is what owner Rena Upitis calls it. It's an apt description of the 204-acre parcel that is so classically Canadian, by turns hilly and flat, part boreal forest and part ancient meadow; rocky outcrops and swamps; a small pond and a twenty-acre, ninety-feet deep, crystal clear and trout-filled lake. Rena bought the land in 1990, intending to build a personal retreat, a place to restore the soul, a place that was mindful of the land, off-grid, and green. She started by building for herself and for her family, a small wooden cabin, perched high atop a hill, overlooking Paddy's Lake.

Rena Upitis is a Professor of Arts Education and former Dean of Education at Queen's University. She's also a mother and wife, a visual artist, a classically trained cello player, and a woman who believes that "no education is complete until you've turned your hand to building something like a cabin in the woods."

In April 2007, Rena was at a conference in Chicago, one of 17,000 delegates, and had spent four days entombed indoors in air-tight skyscrapers when she suddenly had an epiphany – a vision for a different way of doing things. What she envisioned was an off-grid, solar-powered, wilderness eco-retreat, one that would focus on education and community. She knew what she had to do with her tract of rock-ribbed tract of land. Within weeks Rena had settled on a name – Wintergreen – a name that springs from the land and tells something of the spirit of the place. Wintergreen grows wild on the property – a hard-working, useful and attractive plant that stays green year round. Shortly after the vision and the name came together, she put in place a Board of Directors, "People I knew and loved, and who loved me," says Rena, of her Board. She registered Wintergreen Studios as a charitable organization. Next she drew up the plans, and spoke to architects and builders. Then she contracted out the growing of the straw for the straw bale walls to a local farmer. The following year, she was building.

The land was originally homesteaded in the late 19th century by an Irishman named Patrick Nolan. The remnants of Paddy Nolan's attempts to farm the rough Canadian Shield land are present throughout the acreage in the form of stone cairns, old roads, a stone embankment, and some Timothy grass which perseveres doggedly, remembering a bygone era. Rena chose to build the lodge at Wintergreen Studios adjacent to the site of the old Nolan homestead, a place she wished to preserve and honour.

Building Wintergreen without a conventional power source required ingenuity. The huge volume of straw had to be protected from all moisture so as to avoid rot in a summer of nearly incessant rain. The post-and-beam construction with straw-bale insulation necessitated plastered walls. The labour costs in plastering by hand, without the use of power tools, were exorbitant. And because the only road into the site was a dirt lane that could not bear heavy loads, all of the concrete used in pouring the floors had to be delivered in small truckloads, seven of them in total. The list of possible problems at times, seemed insurmountable. Rena enlisted an army of volunteers ages 7 to 83, and she did as much of the work herself as she could. By December 2008, her vision had become a reality. Wintergreen was built.

Wintergreen is now a thriving community; a registered not-for-profit organization, and a year-round wilderness education and retreat centre, offering open houses and residential workshops in the arts and environmental and sustainable living practices. The land houses a spectacular 2500 square-foot, off-grid, lodge, with a dining room, which can seat up to 70 people, and accommodate 20 overnight guests. The lodge uses passive and active solar power, with propane for cooking. Water is drawn from a deep artesian well. Fish and meat are cured in an on-site smokehouse, and vegetables are grown in a World War II styled Victory Garden. In addition to the main lodge, there are several outbuildings including two timber frame cabins (one of which is the original cabin Rena constructed when she first bought the land), two cordwood construction cabins, the smokehouse, a traditional wood-fired outdoor oven and a Scandinavian style, wood-fired sauna. Everywhere at Wintergreen, effort have been made to respect the environment while maintaining the highest standards of comfort and aesthetics.

* * *

My introduction to Wintergreen came on a scorching hot day in July 2010, when I arrived for a week-long writing workshop. I was smitten from the moment I crossed the threshold of the main lodge into the great room that is the hub of all activity at Wintergreen. The cool, stamped concrete floors, the large wide-open space, the tall ceilings, the inviting industrial kitchen, the massive ancient wood stove lying dormant until the cooler weather, the large windows capturing the views of the gardens and out across the land – the juxtapositioning of wood, concrete, wrought iron, stainless steel – and the bookcases full of handsome books, wildflowers in jam jars, a piano off to one-side, an immense, antique Persian rug – create a design aesthetic that is both visually alluring and simultaneously completely functional.

I loved the idea that this land has been preserved and yet is being used and shared, and that by being here, I was treading more carefully on Planet Earth. I was welcomed with open arms by Rena, whom I had never previously met. I felt immediately a kinship with the place and the people. I could hardly wait to meet the other workshop participants, explore the grounds, start writing, get creating, and make my way into that tempting kitchen. Despite being one of the hottest weeks on record in Ontario, and despite the lack of air conditioning and ceiling fans, we spent a glorious week of writing, learning, swimming, and eating beautiful food. I found my way into the kitchen on my first night at Wintergreen and have spent countless nights there since – making friends and working alongside people – many of them volunteers like myself – people I would never otherwise have met.

Food is an integral part of the Wintergreen experience. Part of the joy of this place is the emphasis on wonderful food, and along with companionship and inclusivity. We are attentive in the kitchen, focusing on healthy, accessible, seasonal food featuring local and organic produce where possible. Our repertoire is constantly expanding but we like to cook straightforward, uncluttered dishes, with relatively few, but high quality ingredients. Most of the dishes we cook are vegetarian but we do cook some meat dishes with local goat, beef, and chicken, and wild fish or fish from ecologically sustainable fisheries. Above all, food at Wintergreen is cooked with thought, with care, and with love. Cooking after all, really good cooking, is a true labour of love.

At the end of each workshop or dinner event, the participants invariably comment on how good they feel, and ask for the recipes from the meals they've so enjoyed. It was because of all those requests that we decided a cookbook was in order. Thus, this book, *A Taste of Wintergreen,* was born.

Happy cooking and *bon appétit*….

Lindy Mechefske
August 2011
Kingston, Ontario

Breakfast

Granola, eggs, breads, muffins, pancakes, and more

All happiness depends on a leisurely breakfast.

~ John Gunther (1901–1970)
American journalist

In any case, let's eat breakfast.

~ Isaac Bashevis Singer(1902–1991)
*to his wife, upon hearing that he had
won the Nobel Prize in Literature, 1978*

Wintergreen Granola

Wintergreen Granola

We've tried lots of variations and substitutions, but this basic recipe is the perfect starting point. Mix it up – as we do – try using any combination of walnuts, pecans, pumpkin seeds, cashews, raisins, dried blueberries, and chopped dried apricots. Add the fruits once the granola is nearly cooked, to prevent them from drying out and overcooking. Large flake oats are a nice substitution. If you are cooking for someone with celiac disease, use oats specifically approved for the celiac diet.

Gluten and dairy-free and suitable for a vegan diet.

8   cups quick cooking, organic oats
1   cup large flake coconut
½ cup roasted, salted sunflower seeds
½ cup ground flax seed
½ cup sliced almonds
½ cup chopped walnuts or pecans
¼ cup sesame seeds
1   teaspoon cinnamon
½ teaspoon salt
¾ cup safflower oil
¾ cup liquid honey or maple syrup
2   teaspoons pure vanilla essence
2   cups dried cranberries

Preheat oven to 250° F. Liberally grease two large deep-sided baking trays, or large rectangular cake pans.

Combine dry ingredients, mixing thoroughly. Next combine wet ingredients separately, whisking to mix. Pour wet mixture over dry ingredients and stir to coat.

Spread the mixture on baking sheets or cake pans and bake for about an hour, stirring every 20 minutes.

Add cranberries (or dried fruit) at the end, stirring through the granola. Allow to cool. Store in airtight containers.

Individual Baked Eggs

Like little mini-soufflés, these baked eggs are a treat for breakfast. The recipe doubles or triples easily if you are cooking for a crowd. Best of all, they are tasty hot, warm, or tepid!

Because Wintergreen is off-grid, we work with a propane-fueled stove and try to keep our use of traditional electrical appliances such as toasters, which operate on solar power, to a minimum. So when we serve these eggs, we tend to serve them with some sliced freshly-baked-and-still-warm bread. Heavenly!

Gluten-free.

Serves 6

6   eggs
½ cup milk (can use a milk substitute, like rice, oat, or soy milk)
¼ cup of grated Cheddar
    dash of salt and pepper
    fresh herbs, e.g., chopped chives, coriander, parsley, or dill if desired
    salsa to serve

Preheat oven to 400° F. *Liberally* grease a 12 cup muffin tin or 18 mini-muffin tins.

Whisk eggs, milk, salt, and pepper together and divide between the muffin cups. Sprinkle the eggs with cheese. Bake for 12 to 15 minutes or until the eggs are puffed up. Run a knife around the edge of the muffin cups and slide the eggs onto plates or a platter. Don't worry if the baked eggs lose their puff, that's to be expected and just means you haven't overcooked them and dried them out.

Serve with chopped herbs and salsa.

Panettone Bread Pudding

Serve this almost insanely delicious dish for a special occasion breakfast. It is rich enough for dessert, but works for breakfast, especially when accompanied by lots of fresh fruit and a little maple syrup. If you don't have a Panettone handy, you can substitute Challah or raisin bread. Buy extra Panettone over the festive season and freeze it especially to make this wonderful dish.

Serves 6 to 8

½ cup butter
1   pound loaf of Panettone
¼ cup sugar
3   large eggs, lightly beaten
1   can (370 ml) evaporated milk
1   cup milk
2   tablespoons pure vanilla extract

Preheat oven to 350° F.

Cut the Panettone into ¾ inch slices, and butter. Stack the slices and cut into large cubes. Spread the cubes evenly in a buttered 13 x 9 inch glass pan.

Mix together remaining ingredients, and pour over Panettone cubes.

Bake in centre of oven for about 35 to 40 minutes until golden brown and just set. Remove from oven, and serve hot, warm, or cold with fresh fruit and a little jug of maple syrup. If using as a dessert, serve with whipped cream and maple syrup.

Finnish Oven-Baked Pancake

Finnish Oven-Baked Pancake

Simple, tasty, and sophisticated. Serve with fresh fruit – lemon and orange wedges, fresh berries, or fruit salad. This recipe doubles or triples nicely.

Serves 4

4 eggs
1 cup all-purpose flour
1 cup milk
2 tablespoons butter, melted
2 tablespoons icing sugar to garnish
   fresh fruit to garnish

Preheat oven to 400° F. Very generously grease two round 8-inch cake tins. If doubling or tripling, you can use glass lasagna pans.

If you have a blender, blend together the eggs, flour, milk and melted butter until smooth. If you don't have a blender, whisk the ingredients thoroughly until there are no lumps, and the mixture is a smooth batter.

Pour half of the pancake batter into each pan and bake for about 15 minutes or until the pancakes are puffed up and the edges are browned.

Remove from the oven. Quickly invert onto a serving platter and sprinkle with icing sugar. Cut into appropriate size wedges and serve with fruit.

Savoury Jalapeño Corn Bread

Savoury Jalapeño Cornbread

Cornbread is a versatile dish, which can be served as a stand-alone item for breakfast, simply served with butter and perhaps a fresh salsa as an accompaniment, or it can be served alongside brunch, lunch, or dinner dishes such as beans, bacon, sausages, soup, chili, or stew.

Serves 6 to 8

1½ cups cornmeal
½ cup all-purpose flour
4 tablespoons sugar
2 teaspoons baking powder
1 teaspoon salt
½ teaspoon baking soda
2 large eggs
1 cup buttermilk (or use milk and 2 tablespoons vinegar to make one cup of soured milk)
¼ cup olive oil
1 220 gram jar jalapeño peppers, drained and chopped (*use fewer for a less adventuresome crowd*)
1 cup grated Cheddar cheese
1 cup vegetables (*use any combination of frozen or canned corn, chopped red onion, sautéed mushrooms, sautéed red and green pepper, sautéed onion, chopped green onion, cooked cubed squash, steamed broccoli, chopped, bottled sun-dried tomatoes packed in oil*)
    chopped parsley as desired

Preheat oven to 375° F.

In a bowl, combine flour, cornmeal, baking powder, salt, and sugar. In another bowl, whisk together buttermilk, eggs, and olive oil.

Add the wet ingredients to the dry ingredients and stir until just moistened. Add the chopped jalapeños, cheese, vegetables, and parsley.

Traditionally cornbread is cooked in the oven in a cast iron skillet. If you have a large skillet, grease it and use it, but otherwise a greased 9 x 13 inch pan works too. Bake until a skewer inserted into the centre tests clean, about 20 to 25 minutes. Let cool for 5 minutes, cut in wedges or squares and serve with lots of butter.

Photo by Zinta Upitis

Spinach and Chèvre Bake

Spinach and Chèvre Bake

This dish works for breakfast, brunch, lunch or dinner. It's easy to make, oh so tasty, and beautiful to look at. If you have a bell pepper allergy in your crowd, try making it with sautéed Cremini mushrooms and thinly sliced red onion instead.

Gluten-free.

Makes 8 servings

2 cups red, yellow, or orange peppers, washed, and chopped in 1-inch pieces – approximately 2 medium or 3 small peppers *(or substitute 1 cup of sliced Cremini mushrooms and 1 medium red onion, thinly sliced)*
1 tablespoon olive oil
4 cups baby spinach, washed, drained and lightly packed
300 grams creamy goat cheese (Chèvre)
12 eggs
1 tablespoon Dijon mustard
½ teaspoon salt
   ground black pepper to taste

Preheat oven to 325° F.

Sauté peppers (or mushrooms and onion) in olive oil, over medium heat, until softened, about 5 minutes. Add spinach and cook a further 3 minutes or until spinach is lightly wilted. Place in a greased 2-litre casserole dish.

Crumble cheese over vegetables.

Whisk or beat eggs with mustard, salt, and black pepper. Pour over vegetables and cheese.

Bake until set and golden, about 45 to 50 minutes. Remove from oven, let stand 5 minutes and then cut into 8 portions.

Good Morning Bran and Fruit Muffins

July 2024
Truly excellent. 13

Good Morning Bran and Fruit Muffins

These are the best muffins we've ever tasted. They are packed with fibre and flavour – low in sugar –moist, dense, and filling. As an added bonus, they are spectacular looking. Serve them for breakfast with almond or peanut butter and fresh fruit.

Dairy-free if margarine is used.

Makes 12 jumbo muffins or 18 regular size

1	cup natural bran
¾	cup whole wheat flour
1¼	cups unbleached all-purpose flour
¼	cup brown sugar, packed
1½	teaspoons baking soda
½	teaspoon cinnamon
½	teaspoon ginger
½	teaspoon salt
2	ripe bananas, mashed
1	large seedless navel orange, washed, quartered and put through the food processor
½	cup pitted prunes, chopped
3	eggs
3	tablespoons molasses
½	cup melted butter or margarine

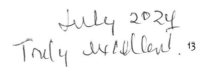

or
} 2 c flour

Topping:
½ cup chopped walnuts
½ cup shredded coconut
½ cup sugar
1 egg, beaten
   fresh sage to garnish

Preheat oven to 350º F.
Combine bran, flours, sugar, baking soda, salt, and spices. Set aside.

In a separate bowl, mix together the mashed bananas, eggs, melted butter, molasses, puréed orange, and prunes. Pour wet ingredients into the dry and mix gently. Pour into lined or well-greased muffin pans.

Combine topping ingredients and spread mixture evenly over the uncooked muffins. Bake 20 to 25 minutes or until a toothpick inserted into the middle comes out clean.

Cheddar, Corn, and Sun-Dried Tomato Muffins

Cheddar, Corn, and Sun-Dried Tomato Muffins

These tasty, savoury muffins, full of protein and flavour are such a great way to start the day. We make ours vegetarian but you can add chopped bacon or ham. These are also great for a packed lunch – just add salad and pickles.

Makes 12

1½ cups unbleached all-purpose flour
½   cup whole-wheat flour
1   tablespoon baking powder
½   teaspoon salt
1   cup Ricotta cheese
½   milk
2   large eggs
2   tablespoons olive oil
1   cup sharp Cheddar, grated
½   cup corn kernels
¾   cup chopped sun-dried tomatoes, packed in oil, don't drain
2   tablespoons Parmesan cheese

Preheat oven to 375° F.

In a large mixing bowl, combine flours, baking powder, and salt.

In another bowl, beat the eggs and oil. Add the Ricotta and Cheddar cheeses. Stir in the milk. Add the liquid ingredients to the dry, stirring only to combine. Gently fold in the corn and sun-dried tomatoes.

Line a muffin tray with 12 jumbo (or approximately 18 regular) muffin liners. Fill the muffin liners to the brim and sprinkle with Parmesan cheese. Bake for approximately 20 to 25 minutes.

July 2024

Gingerbread Muffins

= Dessert muffins

Everybody loves gingerbread and the smell of these in the oven is one of the most heartwarming scents of all. Serve them for breakfast with fresh fruit salad, homemade preserves, and whipped butter. Dress them up for morning coffee or afternoon tea with a dab of butter icing or whipped cream sprinkled with cinnamon.

Dairy-free if you substitute margarine for the butter.

Don't use my jumbo this · just reg. c̄ silicone cups

Makes approximately 24 ~~jumbo~~ muffins

3   eggs
1   cup molasses
1   cup brown sugar
3½ cups unbleached all-purpose flour
1   tablespoon baking soda
1   tablespoon ground ginger
1   teaspoon cinnamon
1   cup butter (or margarine) melted
1   cup hot water

Preheat oven to 350° F.

c̄ Whisk

Beat the eggs, then add molasses and brown sugar. Add dry ingredients alternately with the cup of melted butter and hot water.

Bake in lined muffin tins, for approximately 15 to 20 minutes (depending on the size of your muffin tins). The muffins should spring back when touched lightly. Let cool slightly and serve warm or at room temperature. Gingerbread muffins freeze well if you find yourself with too many.

Cornmeal Pancakes

These pancakes are perfect for anyone requiring a gluten-free diet, and a good change from standard white flour for everyone else. The texture is slightly nutty. Serve with butter, fresh fruit, jam, and maple syrup. Also good with sausages or Canadian bacon.

Gluten-free.

Serves 4

2   cups stone ground yellow cornmeal
½   cup rice flour
2   teaspoons baking powder
½   teaspoon baking soda
½   teaspoon salt
1½ cups buttermilk *(you can sour regular milk with 2 tablespoons lemon juice or white vinegar)*
½   cup water
¼   cup vegetable oil
1   large egg

Preheat oven to 200° F.

In a large bowl, combine the cornmeal, rice flour, sugar, baking powder, baking soda, and salt. In another bowl, beat the buttermilk, water, oil, and egg with a fork. Add to the cornmeal mixture and stir until large lumps are gone, but do not overwork the mixture.

Lightly oil a large fry pan over medium heat. Ladle a large spoonful of batter into the hot oil, and cook for about 2 minutes on each side. Keep the pancakes warm in the oven.

Lunch

Soups, sandwiches, and savoury dishes

It is more fun to talk to someone who doesn't use long, difficult words but rather short, easy words, like, 'What about lunch?

~ Winnie the Pooh, by A.A. Milne

Open-Faced Grilled Cheese with Carmelized Onions

Open-Faced Grilled Cheese with Caramelized Onions

This is a healthy makeover of the classic grilled cheese sandwich. We like to make these sandwiches with dark rye bread, but any hearty raisin bread, or fruit and nut bread makes an excellent alternative.

Because we are often cooking for a crowd, we bake the sandwiches open-face in the oven and finish quickly under the broiler. Don't overcook and therefore dry the sandwiches out. If using the broiler, make sure you watch the sandwiches the entire time. Remove as soon as the cheese is melted and bubbly. Alternately the sandwiches could be cooked open face in a toaster oven, or served as a traditional two-slice sandwich and gently pan-fried.

Serve with a hearty soup and a side salad – green, bean, or coleslaw all work well.

Serves 2 to 4

2   tablespoons butter
1   medium sized sweet onion, thinly sliced in rings
¼   teaspoon salt
1   teaspoon brown sugar
1   teaspoon balsamic vinegar
4   slices of dark rye, marble rye, raisin, or nut bread
2   tablespoons mild mustard such as Dijon, whole grain mustard, or honey mustard
1   cup sharp old Cheddar, grated
2   tart apples, washed, peel on, very thinly sliced

Preheat oven to 350° F.

Fry the onion in butter, adding salt, sugar, and balsamic vinegar. Cook until onion is softened and mixture is browned, about 10 minutes.

Brush bread with mustard and layer with caramelized onions, apple, and top with grated Cheddar. Bake for 10 minutes and then broil lightly at 500° F, watching carefully and removing as soon as cheese is melted and bubbly, and sandwiches are golden brown.

Photo by Japhet Alvarez

Curried Butternut Squash Soup

Curried Butternut Squash Soup

Butternut squash are perfect for making soup – dense, loaded with beta carotene and chock full of flavour, fibre, and texture – you won't need to doctor this soup up with a lot of complicated spices or ingredients to have a stunningly tasty dish. Serve this with some hearty bread and hummus, or a platter of sandwiches.

Gluten and dairy-free and suitable for a vegan diet.

Serves 4

1   large butternut squash (approx 1.2 kg), peeled, and cut into 1-inch chunks, about 5 cups
4   cups vegetarian stock
1   400 ml can coconut milk
1   tablespoon red curry paste

Bring the squash to the boil in the stock and let simmer for about 15 to 20 minutes or until squash is very soft. When the squash is soft enough to mash with a potato masher, remove from the heat and mash thoroughly, in the stock.

Return the soup to low heat, stir in the curry paste, and stir in the coconut milk. Let the soup cook for a further 5 to 10 minutes to allow the flavours to meld, and then serve immediately.

Cannellini Bean Soup

Cannellini Bean Soup

This is a traditional Tuscan soup – simple, full of flavour and easily made. Serve it with focaccia or some full-flavoured bread such as sourdough. Make extra; the flavour only improves the next day.

Gluten-free. Easily made dairy-free by skipping the Parmesan garnish.

Serves 4 to 6

2   19 oz (540 ml) cans of cannellini beans (cannellini beans are the same as white kidney beans)
4   cups vegetarian stock
2   cloves garlic, minced
2   tablespoons olive oil
1   medium onion, diced
4   large ripe tomatoes, diced
½ teaspoon salt
½ teaspoon black pepper
    Parmesan cheese to garnish

Place beans, stock, and garlic in a large pot, and bring to the boil. Reduce heat to a simmer.

While the stock is simmering, sauté the onion in olive oil and cook until the onion is translucent. Add the tomatoes and salt and cook for a further 5 to 10 minutes.

Add the sautéed vegetables to the bean and stock mixture and simmer for a further 20 to 30 minutes. Serve with Parmesan cheese.

Curried Chicken Tea Sandwiches

Curried Chicken Tea Sandwiches

A perfect summer lunch – serve with a cucumber salad and a jug of homemade iced tea. In the cooler weather, serve with a bowl of soup and a big pot of hot tea. Either way, these sandwiches, made with raisin bread, are a winning combination of flavours.

Dairy-free.

Serves 4 to 6

2 cups cooked chopped chicken, cut into very small cubes
⅔ cup mayonnaise
1 green onion, finely chopped
1 tablespoon hot red curry paste
   spring greens
12 slices raisin bread

Mix the chicken, mayonnaise, curry paste, and onion together. Divide equally amongst 6 slices of raisin bread. Scatter the greens on top of the chicken. Butter the top slices and complete the sandwiches. Cut in quarters to serve.

Zucchini Pancakes

Zucchini Pancakes

These zucchini pancakes are unbelievably tasty, incredibly low in calories, extremely healthy, simple, and easy on the budget. They are also a terrific way to use up an abundance of zucchini should you be lucky enough to find yourself with such a thing.

Serve the pancakes with a little salsa, crème fraiche, cream cheese, or sour cream. If you want to make a lunch of them, add some smoked salmon, or perhaps some Canadian back bacon, and a few slices of fresh tomato.

Dairy-free.

Serves 4 to 6

4   cups grated zucchini (about 2 medium-sized zucchini)
½   cup chopped onion
4   eggs, beaten
1   cup all-purpose flour
1   teaspoon baking powder
½   teaspoon salt
2 to 3 tablespoons sunflower or safflower oil

Mix together all ingredients except oil. Gently heat oil in a large fry pan. Drop batter by tablespoonful into warm pan. Fry until nicely browned on both sides.

Ratatouille

Ratatouille is rich in the vegetables that feature in the healthy Mediterranean diet. It can be made ahead and stored refrigerated for up to 4 days. There are an almost limitless number of uses for Ratatouille, and even though we all have our favourite Ratatouille recipes, we include another one here because it appears again in the Ratatouille Quiche.

An excellent accompaniment to lamb or pork dishes, ratatouille can be used as a filling for crepes, or as a topping for pasta, omelettes, or baked potatoes, and is particularly good served for lunch in whole-wheat pitas, served along with toppings like grated cheese, black and green olives, and shredded lettuce.

Traditional Ratatouille recipes call for the vegetables to be cooked separately and then combined. Some recipes call for the vegetables to be roasted. But unless you have an excess of time on your hands, you might like to use the shortcut recipe we use – which still works out beautifully and tastes every bit as good.

Gluten and dairy-free and suitable for a vegan diet.

Serves 6

¼ cup olive oil
4   cloves garlic, crushed
2   medium sized onions, chopped
1   large eggplant, washed, unpeeled, chopped into 1-inch cubes
3 to 4 medium zucchini, cut into 1-inch cubes
8 to 10 medium-sized ripe tomatoes, washed, peeled and chopped (*or you can use a 796 ml (28 oz) tin of tomatoes – if so, try to find BPA free tins*)
1   teaspoon fresh thyme
½   teaspoon each salt and coarsely ground black pepper

In a large heavy-bottomed saucepan or cast-iron pot, warm the olive oil, and sauté the onions and garlic, until translucent, about 3 to 4 minutes. Add the eggplant and zucchini, and cook for another 10 minutes. Add the tomatoes, thyme, salt, and pepper and reduce heat to low. Cook for about 40 minutes or until all the vegetables are soft, and the mixture is a thick vegetable stew. Remove from heat.

Ratatouille Quiche

This appetizing quiche is a departure from the standard broccoli and cheese, or ham and cheese quiche. The flavours work incredibly well together. Use the ratatouille from the previous recipe – just one of the many, many uses for ratatouille.

Serve with a hearty whole grain bread and a tossed green salad.

Serves 6

Pastry for a 9- or 10-inch fluted quiche dish (can use a large pie plate)
2   cups of ratatouille
½   cup of Chèvre, softened and mashed
1   cup sharp old Cheddar, grated
1   cup milk
½   cup heavy cream
4   large eggs
½   teaspoon salt
    freshly ground black pepper
    fresh basil leaves

Preheat oven to 375° F.

Roll pastry to fit quiche dish or pie plate – prick the bottom of the shell lightly with the tines of a fork. Bake pie shell for 10 minutes, remove from oven, and let cool slightly.

Spread ratatouille over the pastry base. Spread or sprinkle the cheese over ratatouille. Season with salt and pepper.

Beat eggs, milk, and cream together and pour over ratatouille and cheese. Using a buttering knife, gently swipe through the custard to draw up some of the ratatouille so that a little of the colour is showing.

Bake for 35 to 40 minutes or until the custard is firm and browned. Remove from oven and let stand 10 minutes before serving. Garnish with fresh basil leaves. Serve hot, warm, or cold.

Spinach and Ricotta Pie

A wonderful savoury pie – perfect for picnics, lunch, or a light supper. Can be served hot or cold. Nice with a cherry tomato salad, and an assortment of pickles.

Serves 6

Pastry for a 9-inch pie crust
1   tablespoon olive oil
1   medium onion, finely chopped
1   10 oz (330 g) package of frozen chopped spinach, thawed and drained
1   cup Mozzarella cheese, grated
454 grams (1 pound) Ricotta cheese
1   cup Parmesan cheese, grated
3   large eggs
½   cup basil pesto
½   teaspoon salt
¼   teaspoon each black pepper, nutmeg

Preheat oven to 350° F.

Roll out pastry for pie shell and set aside.

Sauté the onion in olive oil until soft, about 10 minutes. Remove from heat and add the spinach. Add remaining ingredients and stir to combine thoroughly.

Place filling in prepared pie-crust. Bake for 45 to 55 minutes or until puffed and golden. Let stand 10 to 15 minutes before serving. If serving cold, let stand for half an hour before refrigerating.

Oven-Baked Chicken Tortilla Casserole

This family-friendly tortilla casserole is a good lunch or simple supper dish. Made with corn tortillas, it is suitable for those on a gluten-free diet. Serve with a bean salad.

Gluten-free.

Serves 4

2   boneless skinless chicken breasts, cooked and cooled
1   small red onion, finely diced
3   cups bottled mild salsa
6   cups fresh baby spinach, washed and coarse stems removed
4   10-inch corn tortillas (can substitute wheat tortillas)
2   cups grated cheese (Cheddar, Monterey Jack, Pepper Jack, or Mozzarella)
    Sour cream to serve

Heat oven to 350° F.

Shred the cooked chicken using a fork.

In a lightly greased large deep-dish glass pie plate or quiche dish, begin layering the casserole starting with a thin layer of salsa, then a tortilla, shredded chicken, onion, spinach, and cheese. Repeat twice, ending with a layer of cheese.

Bake in the centre of the oven for about 20 to 25 minutes, until the cheese is melted and the dish is warmed through and browned. Remove from oven, cover with foil, let stand 5 to 10 minutes, and then cut in 6 wedges and serve with sour cream and extra salsa.

Spinach, Mushroom, and Blue Cheese Frittata

Spinach, Mushroom, and Blue Cheese Frittata

Like a quiche but without the hassle and calories Involved with a crust, this frittata is a beautiful dish and a fabulous combination of flavours. It can be served hot, warm, or cold, along with a salad, or just some sliced tomatoes.

Gluten-free.

Serves 4 generously.

454 grams (1 pound) fresh spinach, thoroughly washed
2   tablespoons olive oil
227 grams (½ pound) Cremini mushrooms, washed and sliced
1   onion, diced
1   clove garlic
½   cup grated Parmesan cheese
1   teaspoon dried oregano
½   teaspoon each salt and black pepper
3   large eggs
1   cup cream (10% or half-and-half)
1   cup robust blue cheese, crumbled
3   tablespoons toasted pine nuts or walnuts

Heat oven to 375° F. Lightly grease a quiche pan, or 9-inch glass pie plate.

Cook the spinach until wilted, about 3 minutes in boiling water. Pour into a strainer and leave to drain while assembling the rest of the frittata.

Sauté the onion and garlic in olive oil until the onion is translucent. Add the mushrooms and continue cooking until the mushrooms are browned. Using the back of a spoon, press any remaining moisture out of the spinach and add to the onion and mushroom mixture. Continue to sauté for a further 2 to 3 minutes to cook off any remaining moisture. Remove from heat and stir in the Parmesan, oregano, salt, and pepper. Spoon this mixture into the prepared dish.

Whisk together the eggs and cream and pour over the spinach mixture. Using a butter knife, gently make a few serrations through the dish to allow the egg mixture to infiltrate the spinach. Sprinkle with crumbled blue cheese and toasted pine nuts or walnuts. Bake for approximately 40 minutes or until puffed and golden and the egg mixture is fully set. Serve hot, warm, or at room temperature.

Farfalle with Chickpeas, Chard, and Raisins

This is a pretty, colourful pasta dish – and the slightly unusual flavour combination works well together. Serve it with a big leafy green salad and a sourdough or textured bread. Or eliminate the pasta altogether for a delicious side dish. A gluten-free version can be made by substituting cooked brown rice for the pasta. Crumbled Chèvre makes a nice garnish, unless you are cooking dairy-free.

Serves 4

½   cup raisins *(golden raisins work best, but use whatever you have on hand)*
4   tablespoons dry vermouth or dry white wine or gin
250 grams (½ pound) dry farfalle pasta *(substitute penne or any small pasta as desired)*
5   cups Swiss chard, washed, dried, chopped
1   tablespoon olive oil
2   cloves garlic, minced
¼ to ½ teaspoon hot chili powder
1   cup chickpeas, well rinsed and drained
½   large red onion, diced
1   lemon, zest and juice
¼   teaspoon each salt and coarsely ground black pepper
1   cup pitted black olives, coarsely chopped
    Chèvre to garnish

Combine raisins and vermouth in a small glass bowl and microwave on high for about 30 seconds. Let stand. Meanwhile, bring a large pot of lightly salted water to the boil. Add the pasta and cook until tender, according to package directions, usually about 12 to 14 minutes. Drain lightly and return to pot.

While the pasta is cooking, heat olive oil in a medium sized fry pan over medium heat. Add red onion, garlic, and chili powder and cook for about 4 to 5 minutes. Add the chickpeas and lemon zest. When the pasta is almost ready, add the Swiss chard, lemon juice and plumped raisins to the onion and chickpea mixture. Stir, cover, and let the chard wilt. Then add in the cooked pasta. Stir gently to mix. Turn into a serving dish and garnish with chopped olives, and Chèvre.

Side Dishes

Dips, salads, vegetables

We should look for someone to eat and drink with before looking for something to eat and drink.

~ Epicurus (341–270 B.C.)

Greek philosopher

White Navy Bean Dip

This amazingly quickly prepared appetizer can be made from ingredients kept in the pantry. Serve the dip with sourdough bread, pita wedges, baguette, flatbread or crackers. The dip can also be used to make a white bean bruschetta – just rub slices of grilled French stick with fresh garlic, place a tablespoon or so of white navy bean dip on each slice, top with toasted pine nuts and fresh herbs. Broil lightly.

Gluten and dairy-free and suitable for a vegan diet.

Makes approximately 2 cups of dip

1   19 oz (540 ml) can of white navy beans*
     juice of one lemon (approximately ¼ cup)
3   tablespoons olive oil
2   cloves garlic, minced
½   teaspoon coarse salt
¼   teaspoon cayenne pepper
     optional garnishes: 1 tablespoon olive oil, ½ teaspoon paprika, 2 to 3 tablespoons toasted, chopped pine nuts, or chopped fresh herbs – rosemary, parsley, or thyme.

Drain the beans and rinse well. Place in the food processor with everything except the garnish ingredients. Pulse until creamy with some small pieces of bean remaining, or until desired texture is achieved.

To garnish – swirl with olive oil and sprinkle with paprika, pine nuts, or fresh herbs.

*If you prefer to use dried beans, this recipe will require 1 cup of dry white navy beans, soaked overnight and rinsed well. To cook the beans, cover with cold water, bring to boil, then reduce to simmer. Skim off impurities with a spoon. Cook until tender, approximately 45 minutes to 1 hour. Strain and allow beans to cool before using in dip recipe.

Chipotle Hummus

Hummus is high in iron, vitamin C, folate, and vitamin B6 – and is also a great source of protein and dietary fibre. Bread and hummus served together forms a complete protein, making it a useful sandwich filling or dip. Canned chipotle peppers in adobo sauce are found in the Mexican food section at the supermarket. Freeze the unused peppers for future use. If you wrap the leftover peppers individually, it makes it easy to pull one out each time you want to make hummus.

Gluten and dairy-free and suitable for a vegan diet.

Makes approximately 2 cups of hummus

1   19 oz (540 ml) can of chickpeas
    juice of one lemon (approximately ¼ cup)
1   tablespoon tahini (can substitute peanut butter)
2   tablespoons olive oil
1   clove garlic, minced
½   teaspoon coarse salt
1   canned chipotle pepper

Drain the beans and rinse well. Place in the food processor with all remaining ingredients and pulse until creamy, or until desired texture is achieved.

Baked Jalapeño and Cheese Dip

This fantastic party dip is best served hot accompanied by a sliced French stick. Everyone will ask you for the recipe. It's also amazing served cold if there are leftovers.

Gluten-free.

Serves 6 to 8 as an appetizer

454 grams (1 pound) cream cheese, softened
1   cup mayonnaise
1   cup freshly grated Parmesan cheese
1   200 gram can jalapeño peppers, drained

Preheat oven to 350° F degrees.

Mix all the ingredients together in the food processor, pulsing until desired consistency is achieved.

Spoon into an 8 x 8 inch glass or equivalent sized oven-proof serving dish.

Bake 15 to 20 minutes or until hot, bubbly, and lightly browned. Let stand for 10 minutes before serving with a sliced French stick.

Vietnamese Tofu Spring Rolls

Vietnamese spring rolls can be made in advance and refrigerated until serving time. Make sure they are well-wrapped in plastic wrap so that the wrappers stay soft.

Gluten and dairy-free.

Makes 16 rolls – serves 8

16 22 cm large rice paper wrappers
100 grams of thin rice vermicelli noodles, cooked and drained
1   cup cilantro leaves, chopped
1   cup mint leaves, chopped
454 grams (1 pound) firm tofu
3   tablespoons soya sauce
1   tablespoon sugar
½   teaspoon salt
2   teaspoons sesame oil
2   tablespoons canola oil

Dipping Sauce
1   tablespoon garlic, minced
2   tablespoons sugar
1   tablespoon sweet Asian chili sauce
4   tablespoons fish sauce
     juice of one lime

Prepare the tofu by slicing the block lengthwise into four pieces. Cut each of the four pieces into four long pieces, for a total of 16 strips. Combine the soya sauce, sesame oil, sugar, and salt and pour this marinade into a glass lasagna pan. Lay the tofu in the marinade and turn gently to coat. Let tofu stand in the marinade for half an hour, turning gently occasionally.

Heat the canola oil in a large skillet. Gently transfer the tofu strips to the skillet and allow to brown, about a minute each side.

To assemble, have the cooked noodles, chopped mint and cilantro, and sautéed tofu ready to go. Soak the rice paper wrappers individually in hot water until soft – about 30 seconds. Remove from the water and place on a board. Place about ¼ cup of cooked rice noodles across the centre of the wrapper. Add some cilantro and mint, and place a strip of tofu across the top. Roll the wrapper tightly by folding over the edge and then rolling the remainder. Place on a platter and cover with a clean, damp dishtowel until all the rolls are made. To make the dipping sauce, whisk the ingredients together and serve in a small bowl alongside the rolls.

Pizzaladière

Pizzaladière

Pissaladière is a French dish, typically made with a rich butter puff pastry topped with a mixture of onion, garlic, anchovies, and olives. Our version, served on a homemade pizza base, eliminates the high fat content of the pastry. The pizza can be served as an appetizer or as a main course, depending on how you cut the slices. For a main course, serve it with a couple of hearty salads.

Dairy-free.

Serves 4

Pizza Dough
2½ teaspoons dry yeast
1   cup warm water
1   teaspoon sugar
2½ cups unbleached, all-purpose flour, plus an extra ¼ cup flour
½   teaspoon salt

Pissaladière Toppings
⅔   cup Kalamata olives, pitted and chopped
50   gram tin of anchovies, drained and cut in half lengthwise
1   large Vidalia onion, cut in half and then cut in half rings
2   cloves garlic, minced
1   tablespoon balsamic vinegar
     olive oil

To make the base
Dissolve the yeast and sugar in the warm water. Add the 2½ cups flour and salt. Mix thoroughly. Using the extra ¼ cup flour as required, turn the dough onto a floured surface and knead gently for 20 turns. Place the dough into a large greased glass casserole dish and cover. Place in a warm spot and allow to rise until doubled in size – about 40 to 60 minutes (depending on the temperature). Return to floured board and roll to fit a large generously greased 44 x 29 cm or 18 x 12 inch baking tray with sides. Let stand while preparing the toppings.

To assemble the Pizzaladière
Turn the oven to 375° F. Sauté the halved onion rings and minced garlic in about 2 tablespoons olive oil, and the balsamic vinegar until well browned. Generously brush the pizza base with olive oil, and then spread the onions as evenly as possible around on the base. Place the thin strips of anchovy diagonally across the pizza, allowing about 2 inches between strips of anchovies. Scatter with olives. Bake for about 25 to 30 minutes or until the base is cooked and edges are browned.

Garlic Scape Pesto Bruschetta

Pesto of All Kinds

We love pesto at Wintergreen. We make it by the gallon and freeze what we can't use immediately. It's an excellent way to add flavour and nutrition to pizza, soup, pasta, and fish, and to preserve an abundance of greens for future use. Try either the garlic scape or the baby arugula pesto on a homemade pizza base. Layer the pesto thickly on a thinly rolled base, drizzle with a little extra olive oil, cover it in grated cheese – Asiago, Pecorino, Mozzarella, Parmesan – and bake until the crust is nice and crispy. Your kitchen will smell like an Italian trattoria.

Garlic Scape Pesto
Garlic scapes are ready to harvest in early summer, generally just after the Solstice, or when the scapes have two coils in them. To use, simply wash and dry the entire scape.

36 to 40 garlic scapes, washed and dried, and cut into 2 to 3 inch pieces
½ cup olive oil
2 tablespoons lemon juice
½ cup Parmesan cheese, grated
½ cup walnuts

Blend all ingredients in food processor until desired consistency is achieved. Bottle and freeze, or use within a week. Excellent for pasta, pizza, focaccia, bruschetta, etc.

Cilantro Pesto
2 cups packed fresh cilantro or coriander – stems on, washed, drained, and dried thoroughly
¼ cup olive oil
2 jalapeño or green chili peppers, seeded (as desired) and finely minced
   juice of 2 limes
2 cloves garlic, peeled

Combine ingredients in food processor and pulse until well blended. Use within days or freeze. Beautiful on salmon, excellent on toasted tomato sandwiches, and a great condiment for curries.

Baby Arugula Pesto
6 cups baby arugula, washed and thoroughly dried
½ cup olive oil
2 cloves garlic
3 tablespoons pine nuts, toasted (can substitute walnuts)
½ cup freshly grated Parmesan cheese

Combine all the ingredients in the food processor and pulse until well blended. Use within days or freeze.

Roast Potato Salad

July 2024
Ken, Maureen, Zia,
excellent

Roast Potato Salad

This aesthetically beautiful and delicious salad maximizes the nutrient value and flavour by roasting, rather than boiling the potatoes. Double the number of potatoes you cook – and serve half hot the first night, reserving enough for this salad the next night. We made this salad with goat burgers to absolutely rave reviews.

Gluten and dairy-free.

Serves 4 to 6

3   pounds small new potatoes, skins on, washed
3   tablespoons olive oil
½   teaspoon sea salt
     coarsely ground black pepper
1   tablespoon fresh mint, finely chopped
½   large Vidalia onion, finely chopped
2 to 3 tablespoons chopped fresh chives, snipped
1   cup mayonnaise (or ½ cup mayonnaise and ½ cup sour cream)
2   tablespoons white vinegar
2   small avocados
2 to 3 cups sassy salad greens, washed and dried
¼   cup fresh mint, coarsely chopped
10 to 12 cherry tomatoes, halved

Heat oven to 350° F.

Pour the olive oil into a baking tray and roll the potatoes in the oil. Sprinkle with sea salt, black pepper, and 1 tablespoon finely chopped mint. Bake for 35 to 40 minutes or until potatoes are tender when pierced with a fork. Let the potatoes cool.

To assemble the salad, cut the potatoes into bite-sized pieces. Mix together the mayonnaise and vinegar. Toss the potato, onion, and salad greens with the mayonnaise dressing. Just before serving, add the peeled, diced avocado. Garnish with fresh mint and cherry tomatoes.

Wintergreen Caesar Salad

Wintergreen Caesar Salad

This is the definitive version of the classic Caesar Salad – it is, in a word, PERFECTION. And no raw egg to worry about. We don't bother with croutons either – that way it's safe for those following a gluten-free diet. If there are those with dairy allergies in the crowd, serve the cheese separately.

Gluten-free.

Serves 4 to 6

3   cloves garlic
1   tablespoon whole grain Dijon mustard
    juice and zest of 1 lemon
2   tablespoons Balsamic vinegar
½   cup extra virgin olive oil (plus olive oil to season the salad bowl)
    freshly ground black pepper
2   heads Romaine lettuce, washed, dried thoroughly and torn into large pieces
½   cup freshly grated Parmesan cheese
1   cup shredded Asiago cheese

Prepare the lettuce first and make sure it is thoroughly dry.

Season a wooden salad bowl by rubbing with one of the cloves of garlic and brushing generously with olive oil. Finely mince or mash the remaining two cloves of garlic.

Whisk together the mashed garlic, 1 teaspoon of the lemon zest, mustard, lemon juice, balsamic vinegar, olive oil, and black pepper. Set aside. Grate the Parmesan and Asiago and set aside.

Just before serving time, place the Romaine in the serving bowl, pour on the dressing, and toss thoroughly. Add the Parmesan and Asiago (reserve a little Asiago to sprinkle on top) and toss lightly to distribute.

Wintergreen Sure-Fire Salad Formula

We make a version of this to accompany most lunches and dinners. Mix the ingredients up – our formula calls for four ingredients: (1) lively greens, (2) fresh seasonal or dried fruit (pear, apple, pomegranate, cranberries, grapes, figs), (3) something crunchy like nuts or seeds, and (4) something creamy, like avocado or cheese – Blue cheese, Buffalo Mozzarella, Roquefort, Chèvre, or Feta.

The version below is gluten and dairy-free and suitable for a vegan diet.

Serves 4 to 6

4 to 6 cups of sassy salad greens, washed, and thoroughly dried. We like baby arugula, baby spinach, baby Romaine, red leaf lettuce, chicory, etc.
1   large pomegranate
1   large ripe avocado, peeled and sliced
     juice of half a fresh lemon
⅓ cup pumpkin seeds, toasted

Remove seeds from pomegranate and set aside. Prepare the avocado and sprinkle with lemon juice.

Combine the lettuce, pomegranate seeds, avocado, and pumpkin seeds.

Toss with dressing and serve immediately. This is nice served with any of our house salad dressings.

Wintergreen House Salad Dressings

Nutritional Yeast Dressing
¼ cup nutritional yeast flakes
2 tablespoons water
3 tablespoons tamari
3 tablespoons apple cider vinegar
1 clove garlic, crushed
½ cup grapeseed, sunflower, or safflower oil

Find flaked nutritional yeast at your local health food store. Don't confuse it with brewer's yeast. Blend all the ingredients until the mixture is smooth and creamy. Refrigerate for up to 2 weeks.

Balsamic Vinaigrette
¼ cup balsamic vinegar
¼ cup extra virgin olive oil
2 teaspoons lemon juice
1 teaspoon whole grain mustard

Whisk all ingredients together and store for up to 2 weeks in the refrigerator.

Honey Mustard Vinaigrette
¼ cup olive oil
2 tablespoons white vinegar
1 tablespoon whole grain Dijon mustard
1 tablespoon honey
½ teaspoon salt

Whisk all ingredients together and store for up to 2 weeks in the refrigerator.

Chipotle Mayonnaise
1 cup mayonnaise
  juice of one lime
1 chipotle pepper

Blend together in the food processor, until smooth and creamy. Refrigerate and store for up to 2 days.

Mango and Shrimp Glass Noodle Salad

Mango and Shrimp Glass Noodle Salad

Gluten-free rice noodles, also known as glass noodles or cellophane noodles, are the basis for this attractive and unusual salad. Make the salad ahead, assemble all the ingredients, refrigerate, and dress just before serving. Serve the salad as an accompaniment for dinner or make it for a cold summer lunch.

Gluten and dairy-free.

Serves 4 to 6

340 grams shrimp, peeled and deveined
454 grams (1 pound) rice vermicelli noodles, preferably fine
1   red mango, peeled and chopped in small pieces
4   spring onions, cut in fine matchsticks
½   English cucumber, cut in fine matchsticks
1   cup coriander, fresh, washed and chopped coarsely
1   chili pepper, red or green, deseeded and very finely chopped

Dressing
3   tablespoons fish sauce
3   tablespoons lime juice
1   tablespoon brown sugar
3   teaspoons sweet Asian chili sauce

Bring a large pot of water to the boil, and submerge the rice noodles, return to the boil, then turn off the heat and allow the noodles to remain submerged until translucent and softened.

While the noodles are softening, cook the shrimp in a small saucepan of boiling water for 2 minutes, or until shrimp are pink and plump. Drain. Rinse with cold water.

Place the cooked and softened noodles in a large bowl. Use scissors to cut the noodles into shorter lengths to allow for easier serving and eating. Add the shrimp. Add the chopped mango, vegetables, and herbs, reserving a little chopped coriander for the garnish. At this point you can cover and refrigerate the salad until serving time.

Mix the dressing ingredients together and pour over the salad just before serving. Toss to mix ingredients. Garnish with remaining chopped coriander.

Tuscan Bean Salad

Tuscan Bean Salad

This heart-healthy Mediterranean-style bean salad is a perfect accompaniment to sandwiches at lunch, or a flavourful side dish for dinner. Vary the ingredients as you like, adding blanched, fresh green beans, diced red peppers, corn, marinated mushrooms, or anything else you have on hand. However, this hearty salad is full of taste and looks beautiful just the way it is.

Gluten and dairy-free and suitable for a vegan diet.

Serves 6

1   cup pitted, coarsely chopped black olives
¼   cup chopped sun-dried tomatoes, packed in oil (don't drain)
1   small red onion, finely diced
2   170 ml jars of artichoke hearts, drained and chopped
1   19 oz (540 ml) can bean medley or mixed beans
1   19 oz (540 ml) can chickpeas
2   tablespoons capers
¼   cup pesto *(use traditional basil pesto, baby arugula, or garlic scape pesto – see p. 45)*
2   tablespoons balsamic vinegar
¼   cup olive oil
    salt and pepper to taste

Mix all ingredients, refrigerate for up to 3 days.

July 2024
Maureen, Ken, Zia

excellent & healthy.

Grilled Corn and Black Bean Salad

Grilled corn gives this colourful salad a more distinctive full flavour and a better texture than regular corn salad using either canned or frozen corn kernels.

Gluten and dairy-free and suitable for a vegan diet.

Serves 4 to 6

3
2 cobs of corn, husked
1 19 oz (540 ml) can of black beans, rinsed, drained
1 cup cherry tomatoes, quartered
½ small Vidalia onion, finely chopped
½ red onion, finely chopped
1 cup cilantro, washed, dried and chopped
1-2 avocados (optional)

Dressing
1 tablespoon white vinegar
1 tablespoon olive oil
½ lime, juiced
1 teaspoon Dijon mustard
1 teaspoon sugar
¼ teaspoon salt

Begin by brushing the corn very lightly with olive oil and grilling until the kernels are lightly browned. This can be done either several hours or even a day before assembling the salad. Once the corn is cool, cut the kernels from the cobs. Mix beans and all vegetable ingredients together.

Whisk together the dressing ingredients and toss through the salad, refrigerate for up to 3 days.

Add avocados b4 serving.

July 2024
- has a bit of stock only
at end. 57

Split Pea Dahl

Protein-rich Dahl, a classic accompaniment to many curry dishes, is often made with lentils. This simple version, made with split peas, has a subtle taste making it a perfect foil for hotter, spicier dishes. If you cook a lot of Indian dishes and curries, you may want to make your own curry powder, but for the sake of simplicity, we tested this recipe with a commercially available pre-mixed curry powder.

Gluten and dairy-free and suitable for a vegan diet.

done in medium size pot.

Serves 4 to 6

2   tablespoons olive oil
1   medium onion, chopped
2   cloves garlic, minced
2   teaspoons curry powder
1   teaspoon turmeric
½   teaspoon cinnamon
¼   teaspoon cayenne (optional)
    pinch salt
1   cup dried yellow split peas
2   cups vegetarian stock *+ much more until peas are soft.*

Sauté the onion and garlic in olive oil, until the onion is soft and translucent. Add the seasonings and stir well. *— Takes much longer*

Add the split peas and vegetarian stock and bring to the boil. Then turn the heat down and simmer for about 45 minutes or until the split peas are softened and the stock is absorbed. Taste and correct seasonings, adding a little more curry powder if necessary.

Onion and Potato Bhaji

Bhaji are like fritters, traditionally deep-fried, but in this case, shallow fried in a healthy cooking oil. These are perfect served with Cilantro Pesto (see p. 45). A simple curry mayonnaise can be made by mixing a cup of good quality mayonnaise with 1 to 2 tablespoons of hot curry paste.

Gluten and dairy-free and suitable for a vegan diet.

Serves 3 to 4 as a snack. If using as a main dish, double the recipe.

1   cup gram (chickpea) flour
2   tablespoons rice flour
¼   teaspoon hot chili powder
½   teaspoon ground coriander
½   teaspoon salt
2   onions, finely diced
2   medium potatoes, grated
2   green chili peppers, seeded (or not) and finely diced
1   pkg (300 grams) frozen chopped spinach, fully defrosted and thoroughly drained (optional)
1   cup cold water
Oil for frying – canola, safflower, sunflower all work well.

In a large bowl, mix together the flours and spices.

Prepare the vegetables, and add to the flour mixture – working quickly so that the potato does not discolour. Add enough of the cold water to make a reasonably stiff dough. Do NOT over stir or otherwise overwork the dough.

Heat enough oil over medium-high heat, to cover the base of the fry pan you are working with, to a depth of about ¼ inch. Drop the dough by tablespoonful into the hot oil and allow to brown on one side before flipping. Remember that the potatoes and onions will need to cook, so if the bhaji are browning too fast, turn the heat down slightly – they will need at least 3 minutes on each side.

Place cooked bhaji on a cookie sheet lined with paper towel and keep warm in a low oven while the remaining bhaji are fried.

Dinner

Casseroles, curries, and all manner of main dishes

*Sharing food with another human being is an intimate act
that should not be indulged in lightly.*

~ *M. K. F. Fisher (1908–1992)*
Pre-eminent American food writer

Baked Cauliflower with Ancient Grains

Baked Cauliflower with Ancient Grains

This dish is surprisingly tasty and versatile. You can use whatever grain you have on hand. You can vary the vegetables and type of olives, although the spicy olives provide an excellent contrast in flavours. We recommend making it with quinoa, which is high in protein, iron, and calcium. Serve with a green salad and crusty bread for lunch or as an accompaniment to fish or chicken, or with a chickpea curry for dinner.

Gluten-free if using rice or quinoa.

Serves 4 to 6

2   tablespoons olive oil
1   medium onion, diced
1   clove garlic, minced or crushed
1   head of cauliflower, washed and chopped in bite size pieces
1   finely grated carrot; or 4 spring onions, finely diced; or 1 cup corn; or 12 chopped mushrooms
1   cup jalapeño stuffed olives, or other spicy, pitted olives of your choice, chopped roughly
2   tablespoons tamari or soya sauce
2   cups grated Cheddar (or use a mixture of Cheddar, Parmesan, and Asiago)
3   cups cooked quinoa, bulgar, brown rice, or millet

Sauté the diced onion and garlic in olive oil for about 5 minutes or until softened. Add the cauliflower and other vegetable of choice. Cover and let steam for about 10 minutes, or until the cauliflower is softened but not wilted.

Remove from heat, add olives, tamari, and cooked grains. Turn into a buttered, heat-proof casserole dish and cover with grated cheese.

Bake at 350° F for 30 minutes. Serve hot.

Goat and Mushroom Stew with Blue Cheese

Goat and Mushroom Stew with Blue Cheese

Goat meat is tasty, very lean and lower in cholesterol than either beef or lamb, making it both a healthy choice, and ideal for something slow-cooking. We are lucky enough to obtain our goat meat from a local farmer, but goat is increasingly available in major supermarkets. If you are skeptical, try this recipe with beef instead.

Serves 6 to 8

900 ml beef broth
1   cup dry red wine
15 grams dried mixed mushrooms
3   tablespoons oil
2   pounds cubed goat
¼ cup flour (or use cornstarch for a gluten-free version)
½ teaspoon each salt and pepper
1   large onion, chopped
3   cloves garlic, minced
5   carrots, peeled and chopped
1   pound mushrooms, washed, trimmed and quartered
5   teaspoons fresh rosemary, chopped, plus sprig for garnish
½ cup blue cheese, crumbled

In a medium saucepan, combine broth and wine and bring to a simmer. Add the dried mushrooms and remove from heat. Let stand for 10 minutes. Strain out mushrooms; reserve broth. Cool mushrooms and chop finely. Add the fresh mushrooms to the strained dried mushrooms and set aside.

Heat oil in large pan. Meanwhile, in either a large plastic bowl with a lid, or a sturdy plastic bag, combine flour or cornstarch and salt and pepper. Toss cubed goat (or beef) into the mixture and coat thoroughly. Fry in small batches in the heated oil, until lightly browned. Once the meat is browned and set aside, use the same pan to sauté together onion, garlic, rosemary, carrots, salt, and pepper. Add a little more oil if necessary. Cook gently for about 10 minutes, or until vegetables are softened.

Return the goat to the pan, along with approximately one cup of the broth mixture. Bring the stew to a very light boil, then reduce heat to simmer. Cook stirring intermittently and adding more broth as required, for approximately 2 hours, and until all the broth is used. About 20 to 30 minutes before serving time, add the mushroom medley and continue to simmer, and stir occasionally. Serve in a large casserole dish, topped with crumbled blue cheese and sprigs of rosemary.

Wintergreen's Chicken Marbella

Wintergreen's Chicken Marbella

A version of this dish was made famous by the celebrated Silver Palate Cookbook. The original recipe was probably derived from a Basque or Moroccan dish, since both of these cuisines tend to use the types of ingredients found in most Chicken Marbella recipes. Over the years, the Silver Palate recipe has become something like a jazz standard, a favourite known and loved by all. This is our rendition, which is slightly simpler, but every bit as delicious. Make extra; this dish is even better served cold (or reheated) the following day.

Gluten and dairy-free.

Serves 8

¼ cup olive oil
¼ cup red wine or balsamic vinegar
½ cup dried prunes, chopped
½ cup dried apricots, chopped
½ cup Spanish green olives
¼ cup bottled capers, drained
3 tablespoons minced garlic
½ teaspoon coarse sea salt, and coarsely ground pepper as desired
2 tablespoons fresh oregano, chopped (or 2 teaspoons dried)
16 boneless, skinless chicken thighs
¼ cup brown sugar
½ cup dry white wine or dry vermouth

Mix together the olive oil, vinegar, prunes, apricots, olives, capers, garlic, salt, pepper, and oregano. Pour over the chicken and marinate all day (or overnight if you are that organized).

To cook, preheat oven to 350° F degrees. Place the chicken in a single layer in a large baking tray, and cover with marinade. Pour the wine over all, and sprinkle the chicken pieces with brown sugar. Bake for one hour or until well browned and juice from the pierced chicken runs clear, not pink.

Serve with rice or roast potatoes, a salad or green vegetable, and a loaf of good bread to mop up the beautiful juice.

Cauliflower and Potato Curry

Cauliflower and Potato Curry

This very traditional dish is known more properly by its Indian name – Aloo Gobi. Serve it with roti and chutney, or as one of many curries for an Indian feast.

Gluten and dairy-free and suitable for a vegan diet.

Serves 4

2 to 3 tablespoons olive, sunflower, safflower or canola oil
1   head of cauliflower, washed and chopped into 1-inch pieces
3 to 4 large potatoes, peeled and cubed
1   tablespoon ginger, freshly grated
½   teaspoon turmeric
½   teaspoon salt
¼   teaspoon cayenne pepper (or more to taste)
    fresh cilantro to garnish

Briefly sauté the ginger and spices in oil. Add the cauliflower and potatoes and stir well. Turn the heat down to low, cover and let cook for 20 to 30 minutes or until the vegetables are tender. Stir occasionally and add a little more oil if necessary. This is a dry curry, so do not be tempted to add water. Taste to correct seasonings, adding a little more cayenne and salt and pepper if necessary. Garnish with cilantro.

Butter Chicken

Butter Chicken

The beauty of this dish is that you can make it in a slow-cooker and let it simmer away all afternoon while you attend to other things. Serve it with Basmati rice and warm naan bread, and perhaps a vegetarian curry.

Gluten-free.

Serves 6 to 8

12 to 16 skinless, boneless chicken thighs, cut in half (*use thighs rather than breast meat as the thighs will hold together better in the slow-cooker*)
2 onions, chopped
3 cloves garlic, minced
3 tablespoons butter
2 tablespoons olive oil
2-3 tablespoons hot red curry paste
15 cardamom pods, strung together with a needle and white thread
3 teaspoons garam masala
1 400 ml can coconut milk
2 tablespoons tomato paste
1½ cups full fat plain Greek-style yoghurt
1 teaspoon salt
   fresh cilantro, washed and chopped for serving (optional)

Gently warm the butter and oil together, then add the chicken, onion and garlic and pan fry until the chicken is very lightly browned and the onion is translucent. Place the chicken into the slow-cooker, along with the onions and garlic.

Add the remaining ingredients except the yoghurt and cilantro. Cook on low heat in slow-cooker for 3 to 4 hours. If you don't have a slow-cooker, cook on low in a covered pot on the stove for an hour to an hour-and-a-half. Half an hour before serving time, remove a thigh portion and cut to check that the meat is thoroughly cooked. Check the seasoning and add more curry paste if needed. If the chicken is done, add the salt and yoghurt and cook for a further half hour.

Sweet Potato and Kale Curry

Sweet Potato and Kale Curry

This dish is packed full of goodness – two superfoods – as well as taste, colour, texture, and it is loaded with beta carotene, fibre, and vitamins A, K, and C. Serve it with rice, raita or chutney and onion bhaji with curry mayonnaise. Or incorporate it into a curry feast – serve it with a whole variety of curries, rice, and roti.

Gluten and dairy-free and suitable for a vegan diet.

Serves 4 to 6

2   tablespoons olive oil
2   large onions, diced
2 to 3 small green chili peppers, seeded and finely diced
1 to 2 cloves garlic, minced
2   tablespoons hot red curry paste
2 to 3 medium sweet potatoes, peeled and cubed
½   cup water – more if necessary
5 to 6 cups kale, Swiss chard, beet greens, or spinach, washed and chopped
¼   cup lemon juice
1   teaspoon coarse salt

Sauté the onion, chili peppers, and garlic in the olive oil. Cook until the onions are soft, and then stir in the curry paste. Add the cubed sweet potato, stirring well to combine. Add the water, then turn heat to medium low and cover. Cook until the sweet potato is tender, about 15 minutes. Stir every few minutes to prevent sticking.

Once the sweet potato is cooked, stir in the kale or other greens with lemon juice, and allow the greens to wilt. Season with salt and serve.

Vegetable Korma

You can use your imagination with this dish, using our recipe as a basic guideline and adding vegetables as you prefer, such as broccoli, okra, zucchini, eggplant, tomato, etc. We serve this for dinner along with dhal, rice, naan bread, and sometimes a meat-based curry, like Butter Chicken.

Gluten-free and can be made dairy-free by omitting yogurt and using cooking oil instead of ghee.

Serves 8

3   tablespoons ghee or sunflower, safflower, or canola oil
3   medium onions, finely sliced
3   jalapeños or green chili peppers, seeded and minced
3   tablespoons garlic, crushed
3   tablespoons ginger, freshly grated
2   teaspoons ground cumin
2   teaspoons curry powder
2   teaspoons salt
1   teaspoon ground coriander
1   teaspoon cinnamon
1   head cauliflower, washed, drained and chopped in bite size pieces
3 to 4 large carrots, chopped
2   cups green and/or red bell pepper, chopped
2   cups green beans, topped and tailed
1   cup snow peas
2   cups yoghurt
2   400 ml cans coconut milk
1   cup fresh cilantro, washed and chopped for serving

In a large deep-sided fry pan or saucepan, sauté the onions, jalapeños or chili peppers, garlic, ginger, and spices, cooking until the onions are translucent. Add the cauliflower and carrots and cook until just tender. Add peppers, beans, yoghurt, and coconut milk and cook on low heat until all the vegetables are tender. Just before serving add the snow peas and stir though. Garnish with chopped fresh cilantro.

Grilled Yoghurt Marinated Chicken

The chicken should be marinated overnight (or for a minimum of 4 hours). Serve with lots of grilled vegetables brushed with olive oil and lightly seasoned – portabello mushrooms, kale, zucchini, corn on the cob, small red potatoes, grilled eggplant, etc.

Gluten-free.

Serves 4

175 grams plain Balkan-style yoghurt
4   teaspoons fresh oregano, washed and chopped or 2 teaspoons dried oregano
1   lemon
2   cloves garlic, minced
½   teaspoon each salt and pepper
8   skinless chicken thighs

Cut the lemon in half lengthwise, and reserve half the lemon for lemon wedges. Zest and juice the remaining half. You should have about a teaspoon or two of zest and at least 1 tablespoon of fresh lemon juice.

Whisk together the zest, lemon juice, yoghurt, fresh oregano, garlic, and salt. Add the chicken pieces and turn to coat. Cover and refrigerate for a minimum of 4 hours, and preferably overnight.

Grill on medium heat, brushing with remaining marinade. Cover grill and allow chicken to cook for about 14 minutes (depending on how hot your grill is), turning once. Before removing from grill, check to make sure that the juices run clear. Serve with lemon wedges.

Chickpea, Potato, and Artichoke Casserole

Chickpeas, sweet potatoes, potatoes, and artichokes combine beautifully in this tasty vegetarian stew, which is hearty enough to serve as a dinner. We've served it as a winter dish but it is equally good on a hot summer night with just a simple green salad. If you are making this dish for a crowd (say, 40!), use less vegetarian stock.

Gluten and dairy-free and suitable for a vegan diet.

Serves 4 to 6

2   tablespoons olive oil
1   large onion chopped
2   cloves garlic, minced
2   teaspoons mild curry powder
1   teaspoon paprika
10 leaves fresh sage, minced or 1 teaspoon dried sage
1   sprig rosemary, stem removed, leaves finely chopped or 1 teaspoon dried rosemary
4   cups organic vegetarian stock
4   large potatoes, peeled and cut into 1-inch chunks
1   large sweet potato, cooked and mashed
2   19 oz (540 ml) cans chickpeas, rinsed and well drained, or 3 cups cooked chickpeas
1   14 oz (398 ml) can artichoke hearts, drained and chopped
1   tablespoon lemon juice
    extra sage leaves for garnish

Sauté the onion and garlic in the olive oil until the onion is translucent. Stir in the curry powder, paprika, sage, and rosemary.

Add the uncooked potato cubes and the stock and bring to the boil. Reduce heat to simmer and cook until the potatoes are tender, about 15 minutes. Stir in the mashed sweet potato. The mixture will instantly thicken. Add a little more stock or water if necessary, and stir in the lemon juice.

Stir in the chickpeas and taste to correct seasonings. Allow another 5 minutes cooking time in order to heat the chickpeas through. Just before serving, add the chopped artichoke hearts and stir gently.

Serve in a covered casserole dish. Garnish with fresh sage.

Wild Salmon with Fresh Coriander Chutney

Coriander Chutney is a classic Indian condiment. More like a pesto than a typical chutney, the dish actually appears in several cultures. The South American version is called Chimichurri, while in North America, it would be more likely to appear on a restaurant menu as Cilantro Pesto. The variations are remarkably similar. Whatever you call it – it works well on poached wild salmon and a number of other dishes, including samosas, potato pancakes, onion bhaji, and even served with thinly sliced tomato in a sandwich. You can make the chutney as hot as you like by adding more or less green chili pepper – if you like it mild, remove the seeds and use green chili peppers rather than jalapeños. Add the peppers one at a time, tasting between additions.

Gluten and dairy-free.

For the Coriander Chutney
2   cups fresh cilantro or coriander, washed, drained, dried, and coarsely chopped (*you can leave the stems intact – just get rid of any brown leaves and any particularly coarse stems*)
2   jalapeño or green chili peppers, seeded (as desired) and finely minced
     juice of 2 limes
2   cloves garlic, peeled
     salt to taste

Combine all the ingredients in the food processor and pulse until well blended.

For the Salmon
150 grams of wild salmon per person, fresh or frozen
     fresh lemons, sliced paper fine

If frozen, allow the salmon to defrost all day in the refrigerator. Close to serving time, place the salmon in a large baking pan on a bed of very thinly sliced lemon - skin side of the salmon down. Sprinkle lightly with salt and pepper and bake uncovered at 325° F for about 12 minutes. Test to see if the salmon is cooked; the salmon should flake lightly when you stick a fork into it and should feel firm when the pressed with the back of a fork.

To serve, transfer the whole salmon to a serving platter and cut, but do not separate the portions. Add the cooked lemon slices around the edge of the salmon and spoon the coriander chutney along the top of the salmon. There should be plenty of chutney for 8 to 12 servings of salmon.

Butter-Browned Scallops with Bok Choy

Butter-Browned Scallops with Bok Choy

Bok Choy is an ancient vegetable, widely used in Chinese cooking. It is a concentrated source of Vitamin A and a good source of Vitamin C, and is thought to have cancer-fighting properties. Its slightly sweet flavour works incredibly well with scallops in this fast but impressive recipe. Serve it with rice.

Gluten-free.

Serves 4

2　heads bok choy, thoroughly washed, dried, and chopped into pieces
1　tablespoon olive oil
¼　teaspoon salt
454 grams (1 pound) of large scallops – approximately 24 to 30, depending on the size
2　tablespoons butter
2　tablespoons Thai sweet hot chili sauce
1　lime, juiced

In a large fry pan, sauté the bok choy in olive oil until wilted – about 4 to 5 minutes. The quantity of bok choy will cook down considerably. Remove from the pan and place on a platter to keep warm, tenting the platter with aluminum foil to keep the dish warm.

Rinse and thoroughly dry the scallops with paper towels – the secret to beautifully browned scallops is in drying the shellfish properly before cooking. Melt the butter in the fry pan over medium-high. Place the scallops into the pan and cook for approximately 2 minutes before flipping and cooking the other side. Remove the scallops and place atop the bok choy.

In the same fry pan add the chili sauce and the juice of one lime. De-glaze the pan quickly and stir to combine the ingredients. Pour over the scallops and bok choy and serve immediately with rice.

Photo by Alan Clark

Fettuccine Lindy

Fettuccine Lindy

This is our own adaptation of a classic Tuscan dish. It's a perfect white wine and broth based sauce –delicate, light, slightly garlicky and not cloyingly rich like so many cream-based pasta sauces. It fits all our criteria – simple, full of flavour, and healthy. In addition it's vegetarian. Grazie Tuscany. Buon appetito!

Serves 4

¼   cup olive oil
¼   cup butter
2   teaspoons flour
1   cup organic vegetarian stock
3   cloves garlic, crushed
     juice of one lemon
½   cup dry white wine
1   large (680 ml) jar of artichoke hearts, lightly drained
½   cup sun-dried tomatoes packed in oil
1   tablespoon capers
¼   cup freshly grated Parmesan cheese
¼   cup freshly grated Asiago cheese
     fresh parsley, chopped
     coarsely ground black pepper
454 grams (1 pound) of fresh fettuccine

In a large saucepan, gently heat together the olive oil and butter, and stir until the butter has melted. Add the flour and whisk for one minute, before adding the stock. Increase the heat and add the crushed garlic and lemon juice. Bring mixture close to the boil, then reduce heat to medium-low.

Meanwhile, bring a large pan of salted water to the boil, and prepare the pasta as per the instructions.

While the pasta is cooking, add the white wine, artichokes, and sun-dried tomatoes to the sauce. Continue to cook on medium low.

When pasta is tender, remove from heat, drain lightly and return to pot. Toss the sauce and the capers through the pasta. Place pasta in a large serving bowl and garnish with cheese, parsley, and coarsely ground black pepper.

Serve with a simple green salad and a loaf of crusty sourdough bread or focaccia.

Slow-Cooked Maple Stew

Slow-Cooked Maple Stew

True winter comfort food – the longer this stew cooks the better, as the flavours need time to meld. If you have a wood cookstove as we do at Wintergreen, it's a perfect stew to simmer all afternoon in a cast iron pot. The recipe doubles or triples easily, and is excellent the next day. Serve it with homemade tea biscuits.

Dairy-free.

Serves 4 to 6

2   pounds (approx. 1 kg) of trimmed stewing beef, cut in 1-inch cubes
2   tablespoons flour
1   teaspoon salt
½   teaspoon coarsely ground black pepper
2 to 3 tablespoons olive oil
2   onions, diced
2   cloves garlic, minced
½   cup organic beef stock
¼   cup dry red wine
¼   cup maple syrup
4   tablespoons tomato paste
4 to 6 large potatoes, scrubbed and cut in large chunks
3 to 4 large carrots, scrubbed and cut in large chunks

In a large bowl, mix together the flour, salt, and pepper. Toss the cubed beef in the flour and stir to coat.

Pour the olive oil into the stew pot, and over medium heat, gently brown the cubed beef dredged in the flour mixture. When the meat is browned, add the onions and garlic and continue to cook for 5 to 10 minutes, adding more oil if required.

Add remaining ingredients and turn the heat to simmer. Cover and cook over low heat for 2½ to 3 hours, stirring occasionally.

Blackened Tilapia

North American farmed Tilapia is on the list of the most environmentally responsible seafood choices. But be careful because Tilapia coming from Asian markets is on the list of the poorest choices due to overfishing in this region. For more information on making safe and environmentally sustainable choices about seafood – see Canada's Seafood Guide at www.seachoice.org.

Blackened Tilapia is a FAST, easy, and yummy dinner option. Serve it with rice or buttered baby potatoes and a green vegetable or a tossed green salad.

Gluten and dairy-free.

Serves 4

4　fillets of tilapia, lightly thawed in the refrigerator for an hour
1　lemon, washed and cut in wedges
2　teaspoons paprika
½　teaspoon garlic salt
½　teaspoon dried thyme
½　teaspoon dried oregano
¼　teaspoon dried sage
¼　ground black pepper
¼　teaspoon cayenne pepper

Mix together the spices. Place the fish upside down in a shallow baking pan and sprinkle lightly with seasoning. Turn the fish right side over and sprinkle the top side with remaining seasoning.

Bake uncovered at 325° F for 12 to 15 minutes, or until the fish is no longer translucent. Serve immediately with lemon wedges.

Moussaka

This is an excellent recipe for serving a crowd – you can easily double or triple the recipe and everything can be prepared well in advance. Serve it with a big green salad and bread, perhaps ciabatta, sourdough, or a big basket of buns.

Gluten-free.

Serves 6

	olive oil as required
2	large eggplants, washed, peel-on, sliced in ½ inch slices
2	large onions, diced
500	grams (1 pound) lean ground beef or lamb
3	cloves garlic, minced
1	700ml jar of bottled tomato sauce
2	eggs
⅔	cup milk
½	teaspoon salt
	coarsely ground black pepper
1	cup grated cheese (try a mix of white aged Cheddar, Mozzarella, Asiago, and Parmesan)

Fry the unpeeled eggplant slices in a non-stick frypan in olive oil, until the eggplant is browned and tender, at least 3 to 4 minutes on each side. Push the back of a spatula into the eggplant slices until the moisture releases and the eggplant 'gives'. Place the slices on a baking sheet and set aside.

In the same non-stick pan, fry the onion and garlic until soft, add the ground beef or lamb, and cook until the meat is browned. Add the bottled tomato sauce and set aside.

Place a layer of eggplant slices in the bottom of a large glass lasagna dish. Cover with a layer of tomato sauce and repeat for at least two layers.

Beat together the eggs, milk, salt, and pepper and pour over the moussaka. Cover with grated cheese. Bake at 350° F for 30 to 35 minutes, or until thoroughly heated and top is well browned. Remove from oven, cover with foil, and let stand for 5 to 10 minutes before serving.

Kale with Pan-Fried Vegetables

Kale with Pan-Fried Vegetables

Kale is an amazing vegetable. It is easy to grow, freezes well, and is frost tolerant. It's also loaded with nutrients and fibre. Kale is high in beta-carotene, vitamin K, calcium, and anti-oxidants. Kale is also considered to be anti-inflammatory and is thought to have potent anti-cancer properties, especially when steamed or stir fried (as opposed to boiling which may decrease the level of anti-cancer compounds).

Kale is used all over the world in various dishes, often in soups and in combination with potatoes, with which it teams well. This recipe is fast, tasty, and keeps the nutritional and disease fighting components of kale entirely intact. You can serve it as a main dish, perhaps along with something simple like a whole wheat or sourdough loaf, or team it up with another dish, like lentils and rice, or a filet of wild salmon for a substantial meal.

Gluten and dairy-free and suitable for a vegan diet.

Serves 4 to 6

6   Yukon Gold potatoes, peeled and sliced in ¼ inch slices
1   large onion, diced
2   cloves of garlic minced
2   parsnips, peeled and sliced in ½ inch chunks
1   bunch kale, washed, stems discarded, leaves cut or ripped into large pieces
1   cup of cherry tomatoes
2   tablespoons olive oil
2   tablespoons balsamic vinegar
    salt, pepper
½   teaspoon paprika

Gently warm olive oil in a large fry pan. Add onion, garlic, and potatoes. Cook on medium heat for about 10 minutes, and then add parsnip. Cook a further 10 to 15 minutes, or until potatoes are thoroughly browned and cooked through. Add a little more olive oil if necessary. Season with salt, pepper, and paprika.

Once the potatoes are cooked, add the kale, cherry tomatoes, and balsamic vinegar. Reduce heat to low and place a lid over the pan to gently steam the kale for about 10 minutes, stirring gently once or twice.

Serve immediately.

Wintergreen Bean Hotpot

If you are a purist, you will want to start with several different varieties of beans, soaking them overnight and then cooking them down the following day. For this recipe though, you might just want to resort to tinned beans. Assemble the casserole, put it to cook on the wood stove or in the slow-cooker and then go hiking or snow-shoeing. Come back to a kitchen full of the enticing aroma of a bean hotpot – the tastiest bean recipe ever. Serve it with brown bread and butter. It's also a great winter potluck dish.

Dairy-free. Can make a vegan version by omitting bacon and choosing vegan baked beans.

Serves 4 to 6

1   19 oz (540 ml) can red kidney beans
1   19 oz (540 ml) can chickpeas
1   14 oz (398 ml) can green beans
1   14 oz (398 ml) can yellow beans
1   14 oz (398 ml) can baked beans
250 grams (½ pound) bacon, cooked and chopped
2   large onions, chopped
2   cloves garlic, minced
3   tablespoons brown sugar
3   tablespoons molasses
2   tablespoons apple cider vinegar
2   teaspoons dry mustard

Rinse and drain beans (except baked beans).

Fry bacon, remove, and cook onions and garlic in the bacon fat until the onions are soft. Add sugar, molasses, mustard, and vinegar. Cook for a further 5 minutes. Then add beans and bacon, and mix together. Place in a large 2½ quart casserole or bean pot, and bake for one hour at 350° F. (Alternately, place in slow-cooker and cook on low for 3 to 4 hours.) Check half-way through cooking time to stir and add a little water if necessary.

Goat Burgers with Yoghurt Mint Sauce

We cooked these sensational burgers on the barbeque for 40-plus guests, and served them along with a variety of buns and salads. They were fabulous! The best burgers we've ever had.

Serves 6

454 grams (1 pound) ground goat
½   teaspoon coarse salt
½   teaspoon freshly ground black pepper
2   tablespoons Hoisin sauce
2   teaspoons hot chili sauce
1   tablespoon grated ginger
1   clove garlic, minced
1   teaspoon ground cumin
1   green onion, finely chopped

Make a well in the meat, toss in the remaining ingredients and mix thoroughly by hand. Form small patties; a pound should do 6 burgers. Barbeque until no pink remains. Serve immediately with yoghurt mint sauce and a variety of salads.

Yoghurt Mint Sauce
1½ cups all natural full-fat Greek style yoghurt
½   cup mint jelly
    fresh mint to garnish

Mix together and garnish with fresh mint. Serve alongside the goat burgers.

Photo by Rena Upitis

Pasta D'Amore

Pasta D'Amore

This recipe calls for a large quantity of lovage – a useful easily-grown perennial also known as Maggikraut and Maggiplant. Lovage is thought to aid digestion. Combined with fresh garden tomatoes and white beans, this is an unusual summer pasta, equally tasty served hot or at room temperature.

Serves 6 to 8

2   tablespoons olive oil
5   cloves garlic, minced
1   19 oz (540 ml) tin of white kidney beans, rinsed and drained
450 ml organic chicken or vegetable stock
2   pints cherry tomatoes, halved
1   teaspoon oregano
½   teaspoon coarse salt
½   teaspoon freshly ground black pepper
454 grams (1 pound) rigatoni noodles
10   sprigs lovage, leaves only (about 100)
½   cup freshly grated Asiago cheese
½   cup grated Parmesan cheese

Cook pasta in salted, boiling water. While the pasta is cooking, sauté the garlic in olive oil until lightly browned. Add kidney beans and stock. Cook several minutes. Add tomatoes, salt, pepper and oregano.

When the pasta is cooked, drain. Add the lovage to the beans and stock, cook only until the leaves wilt, then toss the pasta in the sauce. Pour into a large serving bowl and garnish with grated cheese.

Sweets

Afternoon tea treats and traditional desserts

Let them eat cake!

*~ Incorrectly attributed to Marie Antoinette,
thought to have been written by philosopher Jean-Jacques Rousseau (1712–1778)*

Wintergreen Tiramisu

Wintergreen Tiramisu

Tiramisu is the best make-ahead dessert going. This egg-free version eliminates the worry about potential food poisoning from eating uncooked egg white, an ingredient that appears in most traditional tiramisu recipes. We don't think you'll miss the egg – this version is simple and unbelievably delicious.

Make this the day ahead and refrigerate until serving time. Do not attempt to cheat the system and make this the day-of. It is SO much better the next day.

Serves 4 to 6

1	cup Marscapone cheese, at room temperature
1½	cups whipping cream
¼	cup icing sugar
½	cup strong black coffee (can use decaf coffee)
½	cup Kahlua, Frangelico or Amaretto liqueur
1	tablespoon pure vanilla extract
2	150 gram or 5.3 oz packages of Lady Finger biscuits
	small bar of dark chocolate, shaved
	fresh raspberries to garnish

Whip the cream until stiff. Fold in the Marscapone cheese. Add the icing sugar.

In a separate bowl or large glass measuring cup, mix together the coffee, vanilla essence and liqueur.

In a glass serving bowl, preferably straight-sided, begin with a layer of lady finger biscuits. Pour over one third of the coffee and liqueur mixture. Spoon just less than one third of the cream and cheese mixture and using a spatula-style knife or the back of the spoon – carefully spread the cream/cheese in an even layer. Repeat three times, ending with a layer of the cream and cheese mixture. If you have extra coffee mixture leftover pour it across the top layer before you add the final layer of cream. You will need a little more of the cream and cheese for the top layer to get a nice finish.

Cover the tiramisu with cling wrap and refrigerate for up to 24 hours. Shortly before serving, remove the tiramisu from the fridge and sprinkle with shaved dark chocolate and raspberries. Allow at least half an hour at room temperature before serving.

Vodka Berry Sorbet

This simple, sophisticated dessert is refreshing on a hot summer day.

Gluten and dairy-free.

Serves 4 to 6

4   cups frozen mixed berries (raspberries, strawberries, blueberries, blackberries)
1   very ripe banana
3 to 4 oz vodka
½   cup pomegranate juice
    fresh berries and or mint for garnish

Thaw berries for 10 to 30 minutes. Mix with remaining ingredients in food processor, or if you don't have one – simply mash the berries well and add the remaining ingredients, beating well with an electric beater. Freeze in a plastic bowl for 1½ to 2 hours – removing every 15 to 20 minutes to whip with an electric beater (or stir well). Cover with cling wrap until ready to serve.

To serve, remove from freezer and let stand for about 5 minutes. Serve in wine glasses or very small glass bowls with a fresh berries and or mint leaves to garnish.

Rhubarb Custard Pie

A classic piece of Canadiana – this old recipe, or another very like it, has been handed down through the generations in many Canadian families. Many rhubarb custard pies call for strawberries, or crumble toppings, but this version is elegant in its simplicity and the taste is very hard to beat.

Easily made dairy-free.

Pastry for a 9-inch pie
3 to 4 cups fresh rhubarb, cut into ¾ inch pieces
3   tablespoons flour
1¼ cups sugar
3   large eggs
1   tablespoon butter (use margarine for a dairy free version)
2   teaspoons pure vanilla essence

Preheat oven to 400° F.

Line a 9-inch pie dish with pastry and then rhubarb.

Combine remaining ingredients and mix well. Spoon batter over rhubarb evenly.

Bake 20 minutes at 400° F, then reduce heat to 325° F, and bake another 20 minutes or until custard is golden and puffed and centre is fully set. Let the pie cool on a wire cake stand and serve at room temperature.

Old-Fashioned Self-Saucing Baked Butterscotch Pudding

This baked pudding could just be the ideal winter dessert. Baked puddings are typically English in origin and were especially popular during and after the World Wars when food was rationed and some ingredients, like eggs and fresh fruit, were hard to come by. Clever inventive women had to make the most of very few ingredients – this recipe is a perfect example of that. The frugality and simplicity of this recipe belies the smooth, rich, buttery taste.

Easily made dairy-free by substituting soya or almond milk for the first listed ingredient.

Serves 4 to 6

¾   cup white sugar
½   teaspoon salt
1   self-raising flour **or** 1 cup all-purpose flour with 2½ teaspoons baking powder
¼   cup butter (or margarine), melted
½   cup milk or milk substitute

Sauce
2   large heaping dessert spoons (about ¼ cup) of Lyle's golden syrup (do not use corn syrup!)
1½ cups boiling water
1   heaping tablespoon of butter (or margarine)

Mix together the sugar, salt, flour (and baking powder if using all-purpose flour). Melt the butter and add, along with the milk, to the flour mixture. Place mixture in a well-buttered ovenproof 2- litre dish.

In a separate bowl, combine sauce ingredients. Pour the sauce mixture over the top of the pudding over the back of an upturned spoon so that the sauce does not break the pudding apart.

Bake at 325° F for 40 minutes or until the pudding is golden brown and the centre of the pudding is firm. Let the pudding stand for 5 minutes.

The sauce will be at the bottom of the dish and as you serve the hot pudding, spoon the sauce over each portion. Serve with whipped cream.

Tart Fruit Crumble

This is a favourite dessert at Wintergreen. We like our fruit tart and flavourful. You can experiment (apples, pears, blackberries, plums, and peaches all work well) but this version is classic – always a hit!

Easily made dairy-free. We also make a gluten-free topping by omitting the flour and using oatmeal approved for use in the celiac diet. The oats can be whizzed gently in the food-processor to achieve a more suitable consistency for crumble topping.

Serves 4 to 6

2   cups fresh or frozen rhubarb, chopped in ¾ inch pieces
2   cups fresh or frozen cranberries
1   cup fresh or frozen blueberries
4 to 5 medium sized cooking apples, peeled and chopped
¼   cup sugar

Crumble topping
1   cup all-purpose flour
1   cup light brown sugar
1   cup of quick-cooking oats
½   teaspoon salt
½   cup butter (or margarine)

Layer the fruit in a well-buttered 9 x 13 inch pan, and sprinkle with sugar.

To make the crumble, mix flour, brown sugar, oats, and salt together. Cut in butter until mixture resembles coarse meal. Scatter the crumble over the fruit.

Bake at 325° F for 35 to 40 minutes. Serve with whipped cream, ice cream or custard, or just the way it is.

Cranberry Zucchini Loaf

Cranberry Zucchini Loaf

Here's another recipe for the much-maligned zucchini, a vegetable that does not deserve all the criticism it receives. Zucchini is useful and easy to grow; it is low in calories, excellent grilled, essential to ratatouille, perfect for tempura, and fabulous in this recipe – the master of all zucchini loaves!

Dairy-free.

Makes 2 loaves

3	cups unbleached all-purpose flour
3	teaspoons cinnamon
1½	teaspoons baking powder
1	teaspoon baking soda
1	teaspoon salt
3	eggs
1	cup vegetable oil
2	cups white sugar
1	tablespoon vanilla extract
2	cups grated zucchini
1½	cups dried cranberries
1	cup chopped walnuts

Preheat oven to 350° F. Grease 2 loaf pans.

Mix together the flour, cinnamon, baking powder, baking soda, and salt.

In a separate large bowl, beat the eggs, oil, sugar, and vanilla together. Add dry ingredients and stir well. Mix in the zucchini, cranberries, and walnuts. Spread the cake mixture into the prepared loaf pans.

Bake for 45 to 50 minutes or until a skewer inserted in the centre comes out clean. Allow to stand for 10 to 15 minutes before removing from pans.

Pumpkin and Chocolate Cheesecake Squares

Pumpkin and Chocolate Cheesecake Squares

These squares are less sweet than many, and the pumpkin and chocolate are a slightly unusual flavour combination – perfect for an autumn afternoon tea or dessert.

Makes 16 squares

1½ cups graham cracker, gingersnap, or digestive biscuit crumbs
¼   cup butter, melted
1   egg, beaten
1   cup pure pumpkin purée
½   cup brown sugar
     pinch salt
½   teaspoon cinnamon
¼   teaspoon nutmeg
250 gram package regular cream cheese, softened
1   cup semi-sweet chocolate chips
1   tablespoon butter

Preheat oven to 350° F. Liberally grease an 8 x 8 inch glass pan.

Stir together the biscuit crumbs and melted butter and press into the buttered pan. Bake for 10 minutes and remove. In the meantime, whisk together the egg, pumpkin purée, sugar and seasonings. Mix in the softened cream cheese, and beat or stir until well mixed.

Pour the pumpkin over the baked crust. Return to the oven and bake for a further 25 to 30 minutes or until centre of the squares is firm. Cool on a wire rack.

Melt together the chocolate chips and butter and spread over the cooled squares. Refrigerate until chocolate is firm, then score the bars into 16 squares and remove from pan.

Photo by Rena Upitis

Chocolate Risotto

Chocolate Risotto

An astonishingly sophisticated updated variation of the classic creamy rice pudding – this makes a great dinner party dessert. Use great chocolate – it takes so little to make a big impact. We used Lindt 70% dark chocolate and the results were fantastic.

Gluten-free.

Serves 6

3   cups (750 ml) milk, divided in half
½   cup (175 ml) short-grained Italian-style rice
¼   cup white sugar
      pinch salt
1   tablespoon vanilla essence
¼   cup chopped dried apricots
¼   cup dried cherries or dried cranberries
6   oz (170 grams) dark chocolate, chopped
      berries to garnish

Bring half of the milk and rice to a boil in a heavy saucepan, over medium-high heat. Reduce heat to low and continue cooking, stirring occasionally, adding the remaining 1½ cups of milk as the mixture thickens. Cook for about 30 to 40 minutes or until rice is tender and all the liquid is absorbed. If more liquid is required, add another half cup of milk.

Remove the rice from the heat and immediately add sugar, salt, vanilla, fruit, and chocolate. Stir gently, then cover and refrigerate until well chilled.

Serve with whipped cream and blueberries.

Ivy's Date Nut Loaf

This is an old Australian recipe. It is the PERFECT afternoon tea loaf. Serve it thickly sliced and buttered. Irresistible! The quantities listed make four mini loaves or one large loaf. The advantage of the mini loaves is that they cook in much less time, are perfect little gifts, and you can always freeze one for later use.

Easily made dairy-free.

2	cups cooking dates, chopped
1	cup boiling water
1	teaspoon baking soda
½	cup butter (or margarine)
¾	cup brown sugar
1	egg
1½	cups flour
½	cup chopped walnuts
¼	teaspoon salt

Sprinkle the baking soda over the dates and cover with boiling water. Stir briefly and let cool while attending to the rest of the recipe.

Heat oven to 325° F and liberally grease one large or four mini loaf pans.

Cream together the butter and brown sugar. Add the egg, and beat well. Stir in date mixture.

Add the flour, salt, and chopped nuts.

Pour or spoon the batter into the loaf pan(s). If using large loaf pan, bake for 50 to 60 minutes or until a skewer inserted in the centre comes out clean. If using mini loaf pans, bake for 25 to 30 minutes or until a skewer comes out clean. Set to cool on wire rack.

Rhubarb Cake

Spring and rhubarb – a glorious combination. Rhubarb is a brilliant perennial: a useful, determined plant and a free source of food. Everybody should have a rhubarb patch! Rhubarb has anti-cancer, antioxidant, and anti-inflammatory properties. It's also an excellent source of dietary fibre – and best of all, it's so tasty.

Use all the rhubarb you can get your hands on – and freeze the rest for use throughout the year. Rhubarb pie, rhubarb chutney, rhubarb crumble, and rhubarb cake are excellent uses of the plant. This cake is best made with fresh rhubarb, but you can use frozen, chopped rhubarb when the fresh variety is no longer available.

2 cups flour
1 cup sugar
4 teaspoons baking powder
½ teaspoon salt
3 large eggs
½ cup butter, melted
2 teaspoons pure vanilla extract
2 cups rhubarb, chopped into ¾ inch pieces
1 cup semi-sweet chocolate chips
¼ cup crystallized ginger, finely chopped

Topping
¼ cup brown sugar
1 tablespoon flour
½ teaspoon cinnamon
1 tablespoon butter

Preheat oven to 350° F. Butter a 9-inch round cake pan.

Sift the flour, sugar, baking powder, and salt together. In a separate bowl, beat the eggs, melted butter, and vanilla together and lightly blend into the flour mixture, until just mixed. Gently fold in the rhubarb, chocolate chips, and ginger pieces. Spread the cake mixture into the prepared pan.

Combine the topping ingredients, working until crumbly. Spread over cake. Bake 45 to 50 minutes or until a skewer comes out clean. Cool on a wire rack. Serve with vanilla ice cream if desired, although the cake is perfect all by itself.

Dark Chocolate and Raspberry Cake

Some flavour combinations are just perfect – this sinfully rich dark chocolate cake, covered in raspberries, is one of them. An exquisite show-stopper dessert that tastes as good or better than it looks. This is a true special occasion cake.

Serves 10 to 12

1   cup boiling water
3   squares (3 oz) unsweetened chocolate
½   cup butter
½   cup sour cream
1   teaspoon baking soda
1   teaspoon vanilla
2   eggs, separated
2   cups sugar
2   cups unbleached all-purpose flour
1   teaspoon baking powder
1   pint of raspberries

Preheat oven to 350° F. Generously butter a Bundt cake pan.

Place the chocolate and butter in a large Pyrex bowl and pour in the boiling water. Let stand, stirring occasionally until the butter and chocolate have melted. Meanwhile, mix together the sour cream and baking soda and set aside. Beat the eggs white until stiff, and also set aside.

Add the vanilla, egg yolks and sugar to the chocolate mix and beat well. Next add the sour cream and baking soda mixture. Stir in the flour and baking powder. Finally, gently fold in the egg whites.

Spoon or pour the mixture into the Bundt cake pan and bake for approximately 45 to 50 minutes or until a skewer inserted into the centre comes out clean. Let the cake rest 10 minutes before unmolding.

Chocolate Frosting
2   tablespoons butter
⅔   cup semisweet chocolate chips
5   tablespoons heavy cream
1   cup icing sugar
1   teaspoon vanilla

Place all ingredients in a saucepan and heat over gentle heat until the chocolate is melted and the icing is smooth. Pour over the cooled cake. Sprinkle with raspberries.

Old-Fashioned Soft Molasses Cookies

This is a vintage Canadian recipe. Until the late 1800s, molasses was cheaper than refined sugar, so it was popular in lots of recipes like gingerbread and baked beans. It was also a staple ingredient on many farms, where it was sometimes mixed with cattle feed because of the nutritional content. Molasses cookie recipes abound, and there are many similar variations with minor difference – some calling for an egg, some with less ginger and perhaps a half a teaspoon of nutmeg, but otherwise almost identical. This particular version is as close to perfect as possible – a hit every single time we make it.

Makes about 4 dozen cookies

1   cup butter (can use margarine for dairy-free version)
1   cup sugar
1   cup molasses
3½ cups flour
1   teaspoon baking soda
½   teaspoon salt
2   teaspoons ground ginger
½   teaspoon cinnamon

Beat the butter, sugar, and molasses together. Add the dry ingredients all at once.

Roll by teaspoonful into small balls and flatten with a fork on a buttered cookie sheets.

Bake at 325° F for about 12 minutes or until lightly browned. Don't overcook – these are best soft.

Green Tea Cake

Green Tea Cake

A beautiful and slightly unusual cake, with a delicate flavour, this cake is always a huge hit. Perfect to serve after a dinner of sushi and sashimi, or any time a special cake is needed. Japanese green tea powder, also known as Matcha powder, is available at most specialty teashops and in many health food stores. Matcha is renowned for its health benefits, most notably its high levels of antioxidants. Matcha derives its natural green colour from chlorophyll. It gives the cake a subtle but pretty, pale green hue.

Serves 10 to 12

2   cups unbleached all-purpose flour
1   teaspoon baking soda
½   teaspoon salt
4   teaspoons green tea powder also known as Matcha powder
1   cup white sugar
1   cup vegetable oil
3   eggs
1   cup yoghurt (we use Greek style, full-fat yoghurt)
1   teaspoon vanilla essence

Icing:
1¼ cups icing sugar
2   teaspoons Matcha powder
2   tablespoons butter, softened
⅓   cup cream cheese, softened

Preheat oven to 350° F. Generously butter two 9-inch cake pans.

Mix together the flour, baking soda, salt, and green tea powder. In a separate large bowl, beat together the sugar, oil, and eggs for 2 to 3 minutes. Stir in the vanilla. Add the flour mixture alternately with the yoghurt, stirring only to combine. Pour the batter into the prepared cake pans and bake for about 30 minutes or until the top springs back when pressed lightly and the cakes are lightly browned. Allow to cool on a wire rack.

To make the icing, beat the butter and cream cheese together until smooth, then add the icing sugar and match powder. Continue to beat until the frosting is smooth.

Spread a thin layer of frosting over one of the cakes and sandwich the two cakes together. Spread the remaining frosting over the top cake and dust gently with an extra tablespoon or so of icing sugar.

Oatmeal Raisin Peanut Butter Chocolate Chip Cookies

Oatmeal Raisin Peanut Butter Chocolate Chip Cookies

Oh-so-good! Possibly the best cookies ever made? Don't overcook them – pull them out of the oven when they are still soft and just nicely browned.

Makes about 4 dozen cookies

1   cup butter (can use margarine for dairy-free version)
1   cup peanut butter
1   cup brown sugar
2   eggs, beaten
1   cup unbleached all-purpose flour
1   cup whole-wheat flour
½   cup quick oats
1   teaspoon baking soda
1   cup semi-sweet chocolate chips
½   cup raisins
½   cup walnuts

Preheat oven to 325° F. Grease two or three large cookie sheets.

Beat the butter, peanut butter, and sugar together. Add the eggs and mix thoroughly.

Mix together the flours, oatmeal, and baking soda. Add the dry ingredients and the chocolate chips, raisins, and walnuts to the butter mixture. Stir thoroughly.

Drop on greased cookie sheets and bake for about 12 minutes or until soft and golden brown. Let stand on cookie sheets for a few minutes before removing to a wire rack to cool.

Cranberry, Orange, and Dark Chocolate Biscotti

Cranberry, Orange, and Dark Chocolate Biscotti

After experimenting with dozens of different ingredients from hazel nuts to espresso powder to caramel chips, we came up with this rather unique biscotti recipe – using fresh cranberries and lots of orange zest. The fresh cranberries keep the biscotti from ever getting to the rock-hard, teeth-breaking texture of some biscotti. The flavours are incredible together – this is simply the best biscotti we've ever tasted! If you want to dress it up – glaze it with a little icing made from icing sugar and water or milk, and drizzle the icing over the cooked, cooled biscotti.

Makes about 2 dozen biscotti

2   cups unbleached all-purpose flour
⅔   cup sugar
1   tablespoon baking powder
¼   teaspoon salt
    zest of one orange
¼   cup orange juice
⅓   cup canola or safflower oil
3   eggs, beaten
1   cup fresh (or frozen) cranberries
1   cup semi-sweet chocolate chips

Preheat oven to 325° F. Grease a large cookie sheet.

In a large bowl, mix together the flour, sugar, baking powder, and salt.

In a separate bowl, combine the orange juice, oil, and eggs. Add to dry ingredients and stir to mix.

Add the orange zest, cranberries, and chocolate chips, and mix thoroughly.

Turn the mixture out onto the greased cookie sheet – forming a large flattish rectangular loaf – about 1 inch or 2.5 centimeters tall. Bake for 25 to 30 minutes or until the loaf is browned. Remove from the oven and let cool.

With a very sharp knife slice the cooled loaf into biscotti size strips – about ¾ inch thick. Place the slices on very lightly greased cookie sheets, and return to the oven at 325° F. Bake for about 10 to 12 minutes then turn the slices over and bake on the other side for approximately the same amount of time, or until the biscotti are evenly browned and feel firm (and not cakey) to the touch. Let the biscotti cool on a wire rack and store in an airtight tin.

An End Note...

Wintergreen hosts workshops year-round In the domestic arts (e.g., cooking and sustainable building techniques) as well as in the fine and performing arts. In a poetry workshop with Lorna Crozier, this poem was written by Rena Upitis after the Roast Potato Salad recipe, which appears on page 47, was served one August evening to 40 guests. We leave it to you to decide which is the "real" recipe.

How to Make a Proper Potato Salad

Enough of this business with dressings made
of balsamic vinegar and lemon juice
and tiny cubes of pickles and celery and carrot.

I mean, healthy is good and all that. But I say, if you're going to have potato salad,
Suck it up, buttercup: Make a proper one.

Pick the prettiest baby potatoes you can find.
It is best if you've planted them yourself.
You must harvest them fresh from the garden. This means digging them up early.
Don't worry about waiting another month for a better yield.

Try to find all the colours: red, white, purple, yellow. Avoid green.

Saunter barefoot to the mint patch. Lean down and inhale.
Pick several handfuls. Different kinds, if you have them.

Cut the potatoes straight down the middle.
Admire the colours as you chop.
This will make the salad taste better.

Toss the potatoes with the mint leaves and a handful of coarse salt.
Let the salt fall through your fingers
from high in the air.
Then slather the whole lot with olive oil.
Don't bother measuring. Just make sure the potatoes are gleaming when you
put them in the oven to roast. One hour. 400 degrees Farenheit.

Blanket the still-warm potatoes with a full fat sour cream—I repeat: *full fat sour cream*—and mayonnaise, and the sweetest of onions.

Don't forget the chives
growing crazily amongst the Heliopsis (Gr: "sun", "appearance").
Nod to the blossoms as you bend.

At the very end, you must add big chunks of nearly-too-ripe avocadoes. If you're making potato salad for 40 use at least eight of them. Toss the whole thing with cups and cups of feisty greens. Arugula is best. Top with a heap of fresh cherry tomatoes, the best candy of summer.

Cholesterol? Calories?
Taste the salad. Savour that creaminess.
Then add more salt.

Acknowledgments

I would like to thank a number of people for their role in this book, including my family and friends who were often guinea pigs for the test kitchen. Particular thanks to Helen Humphreys whose week-long writing workshop brought me to Wintergreen, and to Elizabeth Greene who encouraged me to attend the workshop in the first place.

Special thanks to Rena Upitis for her vision, enthusiasm, and ability to make huge things happen; and also for her input, careful editing, layout, and design skills throughout this project.

Grateful acknowledgement is made for the following cookbooks, which continue to shape our culinary thinking at Wintergreen:

> *Hollyhock Cooks* by Linda Solomon and Moreka Jolar, New Society Publishers, Gabriola Island, BC, 2009, and,

> *The Silver Palate Good Times Cookbook*, by Julee Rosso and Sheila Lukins, Workman Publishing Company, New York, 1985.

In addition, I would like to acknowledge Kingston-based writer Lawrence Scanlan for his beautiful book, *Harvest of the Quiet Eye: The Cabin as Sanctuary*, Viking Canada, Toronto, 2004.

Thank you to Rena Upitis, Zinta Upitis, Dawson Hamilton, Alan Clark, and Japhet Alvarez for photographic contributions, as noted in the text. Special thanks to Japhet Alvarez for the photograph on the back cover. Thanks to Ken Cuthbertson for editing and other sage advice.

In addition, there are a large number of people who have contributed to the Wintergreen kitchen in various ways. From local farmers, to those who do the dishes, to those who refine and cook the recipes, here in no particular order we thank: Dawson Hamilton, Leah Vine, Karen Smereka, Gary Rasberry, Chris Mechefske, Phil Abrami, Helen Turnbull, Laura Mechefske, Zinta Upitis, Hayden Rasberry, Jennifer Davis, Brian Davis, David Hahn, Marion Watkins, Gerrie Baker, Laurie Gough, and all those many others, too numerous to mention, who have helped out in so many ways, we appreciate you all. Wintergreen *is* a community – a true team effort.

Finally, I thank my mother, Barbara Sutcliffe, for letting me roll out jam-tarts even when I was a mere toddler, and my late mother-in-law, Margaret Mechefske, for all the times we shared together in the farmhouse kitchen. The recipe for Ivy's Date Nut Loaf comes from my neighbour, Ivy Kerley, in Melbourne, Australia. I think of her every time I make it, which is often. And last but not least, thanks to my neighbour and dear friend, Ena Jain, for the fabulous Indian cooking lessons.

Photo by Dawson Hamilton

Wintergreen Lodge at Sunset

Index

A

B

Manufactured by Amazon.ca
Bolton, ON

36044398R00086